CAMBRIDGE LIBRARY COLLECTION

Books of enduring scholarly value

British and Irish History, Nineteenth Century

This series comprises contemporary or near-contemporary accounts of the political, economic and social history of the British Isles during the nineteenth century. It includes material on international diplomacy and trade, labour relations and the women's movement, developments in education and social welfare, religious emancipation, the justice system, and special events including the Great Exhibition of 1851.

The Principal Speeches and Addresses of His Royal Highness the Prince Consort

Initially faced with popular mistrust, Prince Albert (1819–61) fought hard to establish his own role both in public and in his marriage to Queen Victoria. Before he died, he came to be recognised as an influential figure in a kind of dual monarchy, acting as an intermediary with prime ministers and orchestrating the hugely complicated but ultimately successful Great Exhibition of 1851. This collection of speeches, edited by Sir Arthur Helps (1813–75) and published in 1862, was compiled at the request of the widowed Victoria. The speeches reflect the Prince's standing in public life and his unusual position as a consort who was afforded wide-ranging responsibilities. Clerk of the Privy Council, Helps had known Albert personally and his introduction provides an overwhelmingly positive character sketch. Official biographer Theodore Martin's five-volume *Life of His Royal Highness the Prince Consort* (1875–80) is also reissued in the Cambridge Library Collection.

T0371576

Cambridge University Press has long been a pioneer in the reissuing of out-of-print titles from its own backlist, producing digital reprints of books that are still sought after by scholars and students but could not be reprinted economically using traditional technology. The Cambridge Library Collection extends this activity to a wider range of books which are still of importance to researchers and professionals, either for the source material they contain, or as landmarks in the history of their academic discipline.

Drawing from the world-renowned collections in the Cambridge University Library and other partner libraries, and guided by the advice of experts in each subject area, Cambridge University Press is using state-of-the-art scanning machines in its own Printing House to capture the content of each book selected for inclusion. The files are processed to give a consistently clear, crisp image, and the books finished to the high quality standard for which the Press is recognised around the world. The latest print-on-demand technology ensures that the books will remain available indefinitely, and that orders for single or multiple copies can quickly be supplied.

The Cambridge Library Collection brings back to life books of enduring scholarly value (including out-of-copyright works originally issued by other publishers) across a wide range of disciplines in the humanities and social sciences and in science and technology.

The Principal Speeches and Addresses of His Royal Highness the Prince Consort

With an Introduction,
Giving Some Outlines of his Character

EDITED BY ARTHUR HELPS

CAMBRIDGE
UNIVERSITY PRESS

CAMBRIDGE
UNIVERSITY PRESS

University Printing House, Cambridge, CB2 8BS, United Kingdom

Published in the United States of America by Cambridge University Press, New York

Cambridge University Press is part of the University of Cambridge.

It furthers the University's mission by disseminating knowledge in the pursuit of education, learning and research at the highest international levels of excellence.

www.cambridge.org
Information on this title: www.cambridge.org/9781108067034

© in this compilation Cambridge University Press 2014

This edition first published 1862
This digitally printed version 2014

ISBN 978-1-108-06703-4 Paperback

Albert.

From the Photograph by Mayall, with permission.
Engraved by W. Holl.

Published by John Murray, Albemarle Street, 1862.

THE

PRINCIPAL

SPEECHES AND ADDRESSES

OF

HIS ROYAL HIGHNESS

THE PRINCE CONSORT.

WITH AN INTRODUCTION, GIVING SOME OUTLINES
OF HIS CHARACTER.

LONDON:
JOHN MURRAY, ALBEMARLE STREET.
1862.

LONDON: PRINTED BY W. CLOWES AND SONS, STAMFORD STREET,
AND CHARING CROSS.

Two editions of the Prince Consort's Speeches were published by the Society of Arts in 1857; and cheap editions of the same collection have been published since the Prince's death.

The present volume contains, in addition to the speeches previously printed, a speech made by His Royal Highness at the Meeting of the British Association for the Advancement of Science, held at Aberdeen, September 14, 1859; and his address on opening the International Statistical Congress, held in London, 16th July, 1860; together with several minor speeches made by the Prince since the year 1857.

This volume also contains some extracts from a memorandum written by the Prince in reference to the office of Commander-in-Chief.

INTRODUCTION

THE PRINCE CONSORT'S

SPEECHES AND ADDRESSES.

INTRODUCTION.

~~~~~~~~~~~

THE following work contains, with some few trifling exceptions, the speeches and addresses delivered by His Royal Highness the Prince Consort. It is published at the express desire, and under the sanction, of Her Majesty.

It has been thought that this publication will not only be a worthy tribute to the Prince's memory, but that it will have a deep interest for a large circle of readers. There will be those who were personally attached to the Prince, and who will be glad to have a record of these speeches, upon which he bestowed so much care and thought. To the statesman, to the man of science, and to those who care for the social well-being of the people, these speeches will be interesting, as coming from one who himself was a master in those three great

Those who will be interested by the speeches.

branches of human endeavour. And, lastly,
to the general student of literature they will

possess a high value from the peculiarity of
the position of the man who uttered them.
Every free and great nation has had, during
its best times, a long line of distinguished
orators; and, perhaps, the British nation,
from its large enjoyment of freedom, may
defy the world to compete with it in

masterpieces of oratory. The names of
Somers, Bolingbroke, Chatham, Burke,
Fox, Pitt, Plunket, Grattan, Canning,
Sheil, O'Connell, and Macaulay, fill the
mind with pictures of attentive listeners,
leaning forward, hushed to catch every
accent of a great orator speaking upon
some great theme. But in every age there
will be such men as long as England is a
great and free nation. We have them in
our senate now; and we feel that there are
men living amongst us who are fully
worthy to take high places in the illus-
trious roll of British orators. But, without
claiming for the Prince Consort any peculiar gift of oratory, it may fairly be maintained that the world has far more chance
of hearing speeches similar to those of even

the most renowned among the orators just mentioned, than speeches like his; for they were, in their way, unique. It must be a fortunate country indeed, that, even in an extended course of its history, should have two such men, so placed, as the deeply-lamented Prince Consort. Rarity of speeches like those of the Prince.

Now, why were these speeches unique? In the first place, the man who spoke them had not only a scientific and an artistic mind (which is a rare combination), but he was full of knowledge and of suggestive views upon almost every subject. But that was not all. The expression of this knowledge and of these views had to be compressed and restrained in every direction. He was a Prince, and so close to the Throne that he could not but feel that every word he uttered might be considered as emanating from the Throne. He was not born in the country, and therefore he had to watch lest any advice he gave might be in the least degree unacceptable, as not coming from a native. He had all the responsibilities of office, without having a distinct office to fill. At all points he had to guard himself from envy, from miscon- The draw-backs upon the Prince in speaking.

struction, and from the appearance of taking too much upon himself. His was a position of such delicacy and difficulty that not one of his contemporaries would presume to think he could have filled it as well as the Prince did. And all this difficulty, and all this delicacy, must have come out in fullest relief before him when he had to make any public utterance.

Eloquence much furthered by absence from restraint.

It is said, and with some truth, that almost anybody might appear witty who should be inconsiderate and unscrupulous in his talk. The gracious reserve that kind-hearted men indulge in, tends to dim their brilliancy, and to lessen their powers of conversation. What is true of wit is true also of wisdom. In considering the speeches of the best speakers, and comparing them one with another, careful account must be taken of the degrees of freedom of speech which the speakers respectively enjoyed. Often a man gains great credit for eloquence and boldness, when the credit is largely due to his having no responsibility, or to his careless way of ignoring what he has. Such considerations as the above should be continually in the mind of any reader of the

Prince Consort's speeches, who may wish to understand them thoroughly, and justly to appreciate the speaker. It has been said that speech is silver, and silence is golden ; and if there be anything more precious than gold, it may well be applied to describe that happy mingling of freedom of thought, with a due reserve in the expression of that thought, which ought to mark the speeches of men in an exalted position. They cannot afford to make a speech, however good it may be in the main, that has one needless witticism in it, or the slightest touch of exaggeration, or the least indication of party prejudice.

Of the Prince's speeches, as of much of his life, it may be said that the movement of them was graceful, noble, and dignified ; but yet it was like the movement of a man in chain armour, which, even with the strongest and most agile person, must ever have been a movement somewhat fettered by restraint.

The principal elements that go to compose a great oration had often to be modified largely in these speeches of the Prince. Wit was not to be jubilant,—passion not pre-

dominant,—dialectic skill not triumphant.
There remained nothing as the secure
staple of the speech but supreme common
sense. Looked at in this way, it is wonderful that the Prince contrived to intro-
duce into his speeches so much that was
new and interesting.

After reading continuously the speeches
of any remarkable man, we generally seek
to discover what is the leading idea of his

The leading
idea of the
speaker.

mind—what is the string on which his
pearls of rhetoric, or of fancy, have been
strung. And if we were asked what is this
leading idea with the Prince, we might
safely reply—the beauty of usefulness.

Not that there are not many minor characteristics of an admirable kind which it
may be well to point out, and to illustrate

His speeches
exhaustive.

by examples. His speeches, though short,
are singularly exhaustive of the subject.
As an instance, take his speech at the Ser-

Speech at the
Servants'
Provident
Benevolent
Society.

vants' Provident Benevolent Society. " I
" conceive," he said, " that this Society is
" founded upon a right principle, as it fol-
" lows out the dictates of a correct appre-
" ciation of human nature, which requires
" every man, by personal exertion and ac-

" cording to his own choice, to work out
" his own happiness, which prevents his
" valuing, nay, even feeling satisfaction at,
" the prosperity which others have made
" for him. It is founded on a right prin-
" ciple, because it endeavours to trace out a
" plan, according to which, by providence,
" by self-denial and perseverance, not only
" will the servant be raised in his physical
" and moral condition, but the master also
" will be taught how to direct his efforts in
" aiding the servant in his labour to secure
" to himself resources in case of sickness,
" old age, and want of employment. It is
" founded on a right principle, because in
" its financial scheme there is no temptation
" held out to the servant by the prospect of
" probable extravagant advantages, which
" tend to transform his providence into a
" species of gambling; by convivial meet-
" ings, which lead him to ulterior expense;
" or by the privilege of balloting for the
" few prizes, which draws him into all the
" waste of time and excitement of an
" electioneering contest."

Another striking instance of this exhaus-
tiveness, and also of his generosity of feeling,

is to be seen in those passages of his speech
at the dinner of the Royal Academy in 1851

Speech at the
dinner of the
Royal
Academy,
1851.

where he speaks of criticism. " Gentle-
" men," he said, " the production of all works
" in art or poetry requires in their concep-
" tion and execution not only an exercise
" of the intellect, skill, and patience, but
" particularly a concurrent warmth of feel-
" ing and a free flow of imagination. This
" renders them most tender plants, which
" will thrive only in an atmosphere calcu-
" lated to maintain that warmth, and that
" atmosphere is one of kindness towards the
" artist personally as well as towards his
" productions. An unkind word of criticism
" passes like a cold blast over their tender
" shoots, and shrivels them up, checking the
" flow of the sap which was rising to pro-
" duce perhaps multitudes of flowers and
" fruit. But still criticism is absolutely
" necessary to the development of art, and
" the injudicious praise of an inferior work
" becomes an insult to superior genius.

" In this respect our times are peculiarly
" unfavourable when compared with those
" when Madonnas were painted in the se-
" clusion of convents ; for we have now on

" the one hand the eager competition of a
" vast array of artists of every degree of
" talent and skill, and on the other, as
" judge, a great public, for the greater part
" wholly uneducated in art, and thus led by
" professional writers who often strive to
" impress the public with a great idea of
" their own artistic knowledge, by the mer-
" ciless manner in which they treat works
" which cost those who produced them the
" highest efforts of mind or feeling.

" The works of art, by being publicly ex-
" hibited and offered for sale, are becoming
" articles of trade, following as such the
" unreasoning laws of markets and fashion ;
" and public and even private patronage is
" swayed by their tyrannical influence."

How thoroughly the Prince here feels
with the artist! At the same time, how he
demands the highest order of criticism!
What discernment is shown in the comparison between our own time and other
times as regards the peculiar circumstances
of criticism! And, in the last paragraph,
how justly he points out what are the
dangers to High Art in the present period!
Indeed, this speech, taken as a whole, may

claim to be one of the best that have been delivered in our time.

The Prince's desire to get at principles of action.

Again, another characteristic in the Prince's speeches is the evident desire in them to get at the law, or the principle, upon which the matter in question should be settled. As an instance of this I would adduce the following extract from his speech when laying the first stone of the Birming-

Speech on laying the first stone of the Birmingham and Midland Institute.

ham and Midland Institute : " Without " such knowledge we are condemned to one " of three states : either we merely go on to " do things just as our fathers did, and for " no better reason than because they did so ; " or, trusting to some personal authority, " we adopt at random the recommendation " of some specific in a speculative hope that " it may answer ; or, lastly, and this is the " most favourable case, we ourselves im- " prove upon certain processes ; but this " can only be the result of an experience " hardly earned and dearly bought, and " which, after all, can only embrace a com- " paratively short space of time and a small " number of experiments.

" From none of these courses can we

" hope for much progress ; for the mind,
" however ingenious, has no materials to
" work with, and remains in presence of
" phenomena, the causes of which are hidden
" from it.

" But these laws of nature, these divine
" laws, are capable of being discovered and
" understood, and of being taught and made
" our own. This is the task of science :
" and whilst science discovers and teaches
" these laws, art teaches their application.
" No pursuit is therefore too insignificant
" not to be capable of becoming the sub-
" ject both of science and art."

Contrary to our feeling in reading most
speeches, we are always sorry when the
Prince has ended, and we want more to
have been said by him ; and yet, if we look
attentively at any of the speeches, we cannot Condenseness
but see that so much has been said that we of the Prince's speeches.
must acknowledge ourselves somewhat un-
reasonable in wishing to have had any more.
His speech on laying the foundation-stone of
the National Gallery at Edinburgh affords a
notable instance of this. It is so short that
you feel inclined to clamour for more ; and

yet, when you read it attentively, you find
that enough has been said to make up what
would have been a long and telling speech
in Parliament. Happily the Prince's absence from the parliamentary arena freed
him from that tendency to needless ampli-
fication which is the besetting sin even of
the best speakers in the present day.

The sympathetic nature of the Prince,
which enabled him to feel so largely and
deeply for all classes of men, visible throughout his speeches, is nowhere better seen than
in his speech at the Bicentenary Festival
of the Sons of the Clergy. How rarely, by
any one, has a just tenderness for the Clergy
been shown in ampler and in nobler terms
than in the following extract :—

Speech at the
Bicentenary
Festival of
the Sons of
the Clergy.

" Gentlemen, the appellation of a ' money-
" making parson ' is not only a reproach
" but a condemnation for a clergyman, de-
" priving him at once of all influence over
" his congregation ; yet this man, who has
" to shun opportunities for acquiring wealth
" open to most of us, and who has himself
" only an often scanty life income allotted
" to him for his services, has a wife and

" children like ourselves; and we wish him
" to have the same solicitude for their
" welfare which we feel for our own."

In estimating the Prince Consort's
speeches, it is to be recollected that for the
most part they treat of topics of an abstract character, and seldom take up what
is merely personal as their subject, which,
however, is always the most interesting to
mankind.

This could not be avoided from the
position of the Prince; but it is much to
be regretted, for whenever he did speak
of something personal, he was particularly
successful.

For instance, if we were called upon to
furnish for history the main characteristics
of Sir Robert Peel's mind, we could not
refer to any description of that eminent
statesman which would at all compete with
that given by the Prince Consort in the
speech that he made at the dinner to which
he was invited by the Lord Mayor of York.

" There is but one alloy," the Prince said,
" to my feelings of satisfaction and pleasure
" in seeing you here assembled again, and

c

" that is, the painful remembrance that one
" is missing from amongst us who felt so
" warm an interest in our scheme and took
" so active a part in promoting its success,
" the last act of whose public life was attend-
" ing at the Royal Commission : my admi-
" ration for whose talents and character,
" and gratitude for whose devotion to the
" Queen and private friendship towards
" myself, I feel a consolation in having this
" public opportunity to express.

" Only at our last meeting we were still
" admiring his eloquence and the earnest-
" ness with which he appealed to you to
" uphold, by your exertions and personal
" sacrifices, what was to him the highest
" object, the honour of his country; he
" met you the following day together with
" other commissioners, to confer with you
" upon the details of our undertaking; and
" you must have been struck, as everybody
" has been who has had the benefit of his
" advice upon practical points, with the
" attention, care, and sagacity with which
" he treated the minutest details, proving
" that to a great mind nothing is little,
" from the knowledge that in the moral

" and intellectual as in the physical world
" the smallest point is only a link in that
" great chain, and holds its appointed place
" in that great whole which is governed by
" the Divine Wisdom.

" The constitution of Sir Robert Peel's
" mind was peculiarly that of a statesman,
" and of an English statesman : he was
" liberal from feeling, but conservative
" upon principle ; whilst his impulse drove
" him to foster progress, his sagacious mind
" and great experience showed him how
" easily the whole machinery of a state and
" of society is deranged, and how important,
" but how difficult also, it is to direct its
" further development in accordance with
" its fundamental principles, like organic
" growth in nature. It was peculiar to
" him, that, in great things as in small, all
" the difficulties and objections occurred to
" him first ; he would anxiously consider
" them, pause, and warn against rash re-
" solutions ; but, having convinced himself,
" after a long and careful investigation,
" that a step was not only right to be
" taken, but of the practical mode also of
" safely taking it, it became to him a

" necessity and a duty to take it: all his
" caution and apparent timidity changed
" into courage and power of action, and
" at the same time readiness cheerfully to
" make any personal sacrifice which its
" execution might demand."

The Prince's careful preparation of his speeches.
The foregoing are some of the principal characteristics of the Prince's speeches. It remains only to be said that he thought over them with the greatest care and anxiety. His respect for his audience, and also for his own position, made him always endeavour to give the best thought he could to whatever subject he was treating. He looked upon every occasion he had for speaking as affording him an opportunity of saying something that might be useful for his fellow-countrymen; and he toiled to make that something worthy of him, and worthy of them.

The Prince's speech at the TrinityHouse, June 9, 1855.
The Editor of these Speeches has thought it best to give them without any introductory comments or explanations. One speech, however, brought forth so much misrepresentation, that, in reference to that circum-

stance, some comment may fitly be made
upon it. I allude to the speech which the
Prince delivered at a dinner at the Trinity
House on the 9th of June, 1855. It is an
admirable speech, and in it the Prince spoke
out more of his whole mind than perhaps in
any other. Let us recall the circumstances.
We had met with much disaster in the
Crimea. The sickness and death of her
soldiers had touched most deeply the heart
of the Queen; and the Prince, who was a
patriot if ever man was, felt for his country
the tenderest anxiety. Now, let us look at
the speech. In every line of it may be seen
the Prince's intense anxiety to gain support
for the Government, and unity of resolve
amongst the people.

Why does he dwell upon the power of
despotism? Not that he delights to praise
despotism, but that he wishes us to see that
we have an antagonist whose power we
must not venture to underrate. Why does
he speak of " constitutional government
" being under a heavy trial"? Not that,
for a moment, he seeks to decry constitutional government ; but because he loves
it, is devoted to it, partakes that trial which

Despotism strong in war. he points out, and seeks only so to consolidate free government that it may maintain its pre-eminence. How well-chosen are his words when he earnestly asks for a "patriotic, "indulgent, and self-denying confidence to "Her Majesty's Government!"*

Is it any new thing to say that despotism is naturally strong in the field, and in the movements of great armies? From the days of Philip of Macedon, down, through those of Louis the Fourteenth, to the Empire of the First Napoleon, has it not been the object of great men in free countries so to consolidate free governments as to give them that force and unity which should enable them to meet the despot in the field upon something like equal terms—equal terms, not as regards men (for freemen always fight well), but as regards organization, which has so much to do with superiority in military affairs?

---

* When the Prince first came forward as a speaker, some persons doubted whether these speeches could be his own. But the style, the form, the mode of thought, and even certain minute points of expression, might have conclusively assured the critics as to the Prince being the sole author of what he uttered. That use of the word "to" in the above sentence shows that it was uttered by one who had not spoken English from his early childhood, but had acquired the language later.

It seems a needless labour to make any defence of this speech, and a labour somewhat open to the censure conveyed in the proverb that excuse is but a form of accusation; but really the justification in this case is so complete, that it does not come within the meaning of the word "excuse." Every lover of this free country must perceive that its only danger of being worsted in some great contest is a momentary inferiority as regards organization; and we should feel much gratitude to any one who, in an exalted position, has the loving boldness to point out what are our dangers. The Prince asked for confidence in the Government. England gave that confidence, and the cause was won. *Danger from want of organization.*

Perhaps the greatest injury that men highly-placed can do their countrymen is to flatter them, and to hide from them any point of weakness that there may be in the nation. We smile at flattery when addressed to private persons, and think it no great harm; but it swells into a mischief of gigantic magnitude when addressed to a nation by those who enjoy its confidence. *The fearful mischief of flattering a nation.*

We have not far to look for instances

of nations being brought to the brink of
ruin because they have not had public men
to tell them stern truths as to the ineffi-
ciency of their means, and the unwisdom
of their ends. All honour, then, to the
man who has the courage, at a critical
moment, to tell his countrymen where their
peril really lies, and what difficulties they
must be prepared to overcome.

A view of the Prince's character.

It may, perhaps, be not unwelcome to
the reader, and not inappropriate to the
subject, that, as an addition to this Introduction, I should attempt to give some view
of the character of the Prince, having had
some opportunities of observing him closely
during the last year or two of his life, and
having since heard and carefully compared
what those who knew him best could tell of
him. Such an attempt to depict the Prince's
character may be useful to the future histo-
rian, who has to bring before himself some
distinct image of each remarkable man he
writes about, and who, for the most part,
is furnished with only a superficial description, made up of the ordinary epithets

which are attached, in a very haphazard
way, to the various qualities of eminent
persons by their contemporaries. We really
obtain very little notion of a creature so
strangely-complex as a man, when we are
told of him that he was virtuous, that he
was just, that he loved the Arts, and that
he was good in all the important relations
of life. We still hunger to know what
were his peculiarities, and what made him
differ from other men; for each man, after
all, is a sort of new and distinct creation.

It is a great advantage, in estimating any
character, to have a clear idea of the aspect
of the person whose character is drawn.
There are, fortunately, many portraits of the
Prince Consort which possess considerable
merit; still there is something about almost
every countenance which no portrait can
adequately convey, and which must be left
to description.

The Prince had a noble presence. His
carriage was erect: his figure betokened
strength and activity; and his demeanour
was dignified. He had a staid, earnest,
thoughtful look when he was in a grave

A description
of the Prince's
personal
appearance.

mood; but when he smiled (and this is
what no portrait can tell of a man) his
whole countenance was irradiated with pleasure; and there was a pleasant sound and
a heartiness about his laugh which will not
soon be forgotten by those who were wont
to hear it.

He was very handsome as a young man;
but, as often happens with thoughtful men
who go through a good deal, his face grew
to be a finer face than the early portraits of
him promised; and his countenance never
assumed a nobler aspect, nor had more real
beauty in it, than in the last year or two of
his life.

The character is written in the countenance, however difficult it may be to deci-
pher; and in the Prince's face there were
none of those fatal lines which indicate craft
or insincerity, greed or sensuality; but all
was clear, open, pure-minded, and honest.
Marks of thought, of care, of studiousness,
were there; but they were accompanied by
signs of a soul at peace with itself, and
which was troubled chiefly by its love for
others, and its solicitude for their welfare.

Perhaps the thing of all others that struck an observer most when he came to see the Prince nearly, was the originality of his mind; and it was an originality divested from all eccentricity. He would insist on thinking his own thoughts upon every subject that came before him; and, whether he arrived at the same results as other men, or gainsaid them, his conclusions were always adopted upon laborious reasonings of his own.

The originality of the Prince.

The next striking peculiarity about the Prince was his extreme quickness—intellectually speaking. He was one of those men who seem always to have all their powers of thought at hand, and all their knowledge readily producible.

The quickness of his intellect.

In serious conversation he was perhaps the first man of his day. He was a very sincere person in his way of talking; so that, when he spoke at all upon any subject, he never played with it: he never took one side of a question because the person he was conversing with had taken the other: and, in fact, earnest discussion was one of his greatest enjoyments. He was very patient

His merits in conversation.

His tolerance of contradiction.

in bearing criticism and contradiction; and, indeed, rather liked to be opposed, so that from opposition he might elicit truth, which was always his first object.

Fond of wit and humour.

He delighted in wit and humour; and, in his narration of what was ludicrous, threw just so much of imitation into it as would enable you to bring the scene vividly before you, without at the same time making his imitation in the least degree ungraceful.

His love of freedom.

There have been few men who have had a greater love of freedom, in its deepest and in its widest sense, than the Prince Consort. Indeed, in this respect he was even more English than the English themselves.

His sense of duty.

A strong characteristic of the Prince's mind was its sense of duty. He was sure to go rigidly through anything he had undertaken to do; and he was one of those few men into whose minds questions of self-interest never enter, or are absolutely ignored, when the paramount obligation of duty is presented to them. If he had been a sovereign prince, and, in a moment of peril, had adopted a form of constitution which was opposed to his inclination or his judgment, he would still have abided by it strictly when quiet times came; and the change, if change there was to be, must have come from the other parties to the contract, and not from him. He was too great a man to wish to rule, if the power was to be purchased by anything having the reality, or even the semblance, of dishonour. It is not too much to say, that, if he had been placed in the position of Washington, he could have played the part of Washington, taking what honour and power his fellow-citizens were pleased to give him, and not asking, or scheming, for any more. He must have sympathized much with the late Duke of Wellington, whose main idea seemed to be to get through life justly and creditably, taking the full measure of responsibility put upon him, and not seeking to have his soul burdened with any more. Such men are absolutely of a different order of mind from the commonplace seekers after power and self-glorification.

The Prince, as all know, was a man of many pursuits and of various accomplishments, with an ardent admiration for the beautiful both in Nature and in Art.

The Prince gradually gave up some of his favourite pursuits.
Gradually, however, he gave up pursuits that he was fond of, such as the cultivation of music and drawing; not that he relished these pursuits less than heretofore, but that he felt it was incumbent upon him to attend more and more to business. He was not to employ himself upon what specially delighted him, but to attend to what it was his duty to attend to. And there was not time for both.

Another characteristic of the Prince (which is not always found in those who take a strict view of duty) was his strong aversion to anything like prejudice or in-
The Prince's aversion to prejudice and intolerance.
tolerance. He loved to keep his own mind clear for the reception of new facts and arguments; and he rather expected that everybody else should do the same. His mind was eminently judicial; and it was never too late to bring him any new view, or fresh fact, which might be made to bear upon the ultimate decision which he would have to give upon the matter. To investigate carefully, weigh patiently, discuss dispassionately, and then, not swiftly, but after much turning over the question in his mind,

to come to a decision—was his usual mode
of procedure in all matters of much moment.

There was one very rare quality to be
noticed in the Prince, — that he had the
greatest delight in anybody else saying a
fine saying, or doing a great deed. He
would rejoice over it, and talk about it, for
days ; and whether it was a thing nobly
said or done by a little child, or by a veteran
statesman, it gave him equal pleasure. He
delighted in humanity doing well on any
occasion and in any manner.

The Prince's
delight in the
good deeds of
other persons.

This is surely very uncommon. We
meet with people who can say fine sayings,
and even do noble actions, but who are not
very fond of dwelling upon the great
sayings or noble deeds of other persons.
But, indeed, throughout his career, the
Prince was one of those who threw his life
into other people's lives, and lived in them.
And never was there an instance of more
unselfish and chivalrous devotion than that
of his to his Consort-Sovereign and to his
adopted country. That Her reign might
be great and glorious ; that his adopted
country might excel in art, in science, in

literature, and, what was dearer still to him, in social well-being, formed ever his chief hope and aim. And he would have been contented to have been very obscure, if these high aims and objects could in the least degree have thereby been furthered and secured.

This love of his adopted country did not prevent his being exceedingly attached to his birthplace and his native country. He would recur in the most touching manner, and with childlike joy, to all the reminiscences of his happy childhood. But, indeed, it is clear that, throughout his life, he became in a certain measure attached to every place where he dwelt. This is natural, as he always sought to improve the people and the place where he lived; and so, inevitably, he became attached to it and to them.

A biographer who has some very beautiful character to describe, and who knows the unwillingness that there is in the world to accept, without much qualification, great praise of any human being, will almost be glad to have any small defect to note in

The Prince's love of his birthplace.

his hero. It gives some relief to the picture, and it adds verisimilitude. This defect (if so it can be called) in the Prince consisted in a certain appearance of shyness which he never conquered. And, in truth, it may be questioned whether it is a thing that can be conquered, though large converse with the world may enable a man to conceal it. Much might be said to explain and justify this shyness in the Prince; but there it was, and no doubt it sometimes prevented his high qualities from being at once observed and fully estimated. It was the shyness of a very delicate nature, that is not sure it will please, and is without the confidence and the vanity which often go to form characters that are outwardly more genial.

The Prince's shyness.

The causes of it.

The effect of this shyness was heightened by the rigid sincerity which marked the Prince's character. There are some men who gain much popularity by always expressing in a hearty manner much more than they feel. They are "*delighted*" to see you; they "*rejoice*" to hear that your health is improving; and you, not caring to inquire how much substance there is behind these phrases, and not disinclined to imagine that your health is a matter of importance which people might naturally take interest in, enjoy this hearty but somewhat inflated welcome. But from the Prince there were no phrases of this kind to be had : nothing that was not based upon clear and complete sincerity. Indeed, his refined nature shrank from expressing all it felt, and still less would it condescend to put on any semblance of feeling which was not backed up by complete reality.

The Prince's temperament.

It is very difficult to describe a man's temperament, especially when it is of a somewhat complex nature, as was that of the Prince. It was a buoyant, joyous, happy temperament. It made his home and his household glad. To use a common expression, but a forcible one, he was "the life " and soul of the house." Moreover, the Prince's temperament was very equable, not subject to sudden elations or depressions. To illustrate, however, the complexity, before alluded to, of men's temperaments— beneath this joyousness of the Prince, deep down in the character, there was a vein, not exactly of melancholy, but certainly of pensiveness, which grew a little more sombre as the years went on. It was a pensiveness bred from much pondering upon the difficulty of human affairs, and upon the serious thing that life is.

The writer of this Introduction has often, in his imagination, divided men into two great classes, which seem to him separated by a wide gulf of thought and feeling. The one class is, if it may be so expressed, on the side of humanity : the other is opposed or indifferent to it. This essential difference of character is not necessarily the effect or the concomitant of virtue or of vice, of hopefulness or despondency, of a love of justice or a proneness to injustice ; and it has still less to do with any of the intellectual qualities. But it depends upon the presence or the absence of a large and loving nature, where the lovingness takes heed of all humanity. The Prince was preeminently one of the first class. He wished for success to all honest human endeavour. No love of criticism, no fondness for paradox, no desire to exalt his own opinion, made him waver in his yearning for the

A division of mankind into two classes.

good of humanity. This caused his intense

The Prince's
sympathy
for work.

sympathy with all human work, from that of the artisan to that of the statesman. We have in this age used the word "philan- " thropy " till we are tired of it, till it has become a mawkish word with us; but still

The Prince a
philanthro-
pist.

there is something very beautiful correspond- ing to that word, and that was what the Prince possessed. We all recognize in our respective spheres the distinction I have drawn above between these two classes. We all know, for instance, when any public or private disaster happens, who will really grieve over it and endeavour to retrieve it; and who will make it a subject for vain comment, pretended lamentation, or boasting censure. And a nation, like a man, would

The Prince
helpful in
times of
trouble.

have come to the Prince when in real trouble, and have found in him one whose sole thought would have been, "what can " now be done for the best ? " For he was, as I said before, pre-eminently on the side of humanity, and all that touched other men, touched him, too, very nearly.

His aversion
to flattery.

The Prince had a horror of flattery. I use the word " horror " advisedly. Dr. Johnson somewhere says that flattery shows, at any rate, a desire to please, and may, therefore, be estimated as worth something on that account. But the Prince could not view it in that light. He shuddered at it: he tried to get away from it as soon as he could. It was simply nauseous to him.

He had the same feeling with regard to vice generally. Its presence depressed him, grieved him, horrified him. His tolerance allowed him to make excuses for the vices of individual men; but the evil itself he hated. *His aversion to vice.*

What, however, was especially repugnant to the Prince was lowness. He could not bear men to be actuated by low motives. A remarkably unselfish man himself, he scarcely understood selfishness in others; and, when he recognized it, he felt an abhorrence for it. The conditions that the Prince drew up for the prize that is given by Her Majesty at Wellington College are very characteristic of him. This prize is not to be awarded to the most bookish boy, to the least faulty boy, to the boy who should be most precise, diligent, and prudent; but to the noblest boy, to the boy *Low motives odious to him.*

who should afford most promise of becoming a large-hearted, high-motived man.

The Prince was a deeply religious man, yet was entirely free from the faintest tinge of bigotry or sectarianism. His strong faith in the great truths of religion coexisted with a breadth of tolerance for other men struggling in their various ways to attain those truths. His views of Religion did not lead him to separate himself from other men ; and in these high matters he rather sought to find unity in diversity, than to magnify small differences. Thus he endeavoured to associate himself with all earnest seekers after religious truth.

The Prince's religious feelings.

It must have occurred to every observer of mankind to notice that there are persons who acquire knowledge without loving it. They have read all the noblest works in literature without being profoundly touched by any of them. They may be excellent classical scholars, and yet they do not seem to love their Horace or their Virgil. Their minds are not penetrated with a sense of the beauty of these authors. They do not see that an idea has been expressed once

Some men acquire knowledge without loving it.

and for ever, in the choicest language, by
these masters of expression : whereas, some
humble student perceives all this ; and
Virgil, Horace, and Ovid belong to him.
The same thing occurs in science ; the same
in law ; the same in medicine. You see men
who know all about their art, or their
science, but who do not seem to love it.
They are not led up to all nature by it.
It is with them a business, rather than a
science or an art. Such was not the case
with the Prince. He was singularly im-
pressed with the intellectual beauty of
knowledge ; for, as he once remarked to
Her who most sympathised with him,
" To me, a long, closely-connected train
" of reasoning is like a beautiful strain
" of music. You can hardly imagine my
" delight in it." But this was not all with
him. He was one of those rare seekers
after truth who carry their affections into
their acquisitions of knowledge. He loved
knowledge on account of what it could do
for mankind ; and no man of our time sympathized more intimately with that splendid
outburst of Bacon, where the great Chan-
cellor exclaims,—

" Knowledge is not a couch, whereupon
" to rest a searching and restless spirit; or
" a terrace for a wandering and variable
" mind to walk up and down with a fair
" prospect; or a tower of state for a proud
" mind to raise itself upon; or a fort or
" commanding ground for strife and con-
" tention; or a shop for profit or sale; but
" a rich storehouse for the glory of the
" Creator, and the relief of man's estate.
" But this is that which will indeed dignify
" and exalt knowledge, if contemplation
" and action may be more nearly and
" straitly conjoined and united together
" than they have been; a conjunction like
" unto that of the two highest planets—
" Saturn, the planet of rest and contem-
" plation, and Jupiter, the planet of civil
" society and action."

It was with a feeling similar to that expressed in the foregoing passage that the
Prince would comment, for instance, upon
an improvement in manufacture, as bearing,
especially, upon the health and strength
of the poorest classes. It was for " the
" relief of Man's estate" that this amiable

Prince delighted most in the extension of the bounds of knowledge.

It is always a subject of interest to endeavour to find out how men who have been remarkable for knowledge have found time and opportunity, in this busy, anxious, hurried world, to acquire that knowledge. And in the case of the Prince it is especially difficult to answer the question. But the truth is, that, much as the Prince read books (and in early life he had been very studious), he read men and Nature more. He never gave a listless or half-awake attention to anything that he thought worth looking at, or to any person to whom he thought it worth while to listen. And to the observant man, who is always on the watch for general laws, the minutest objects contemplated by him are full of insight and instruction. In the Prince's converse with men, he delighted at getting at what they knew best, and what they could do. He would always try to get from them the mystery of their craft ; and, probably, after the Prince had had an interview with any person of intelligence, that

How the Prince acquired knowledge.

person went away having learnt something
from the Prince, and the Prince having
learnt something from him. Such men,
who are always on the alert to gain and to
impart knowledge, deserve to know; and
their knowledge soon grows to be beyond
book-knowledge, and enters into a higher
sphere, as being the result of delicate and
attentive observation made by themselves,
and for themselves. This is how I account
for the Prince's remarkable acquisition of
much and various knowledge.

If any man in England cared for the
working classes, it was the Prince. He
understood the great difficulty of the time
as regards these classes; namely, the providing for them fitting habitations. He
was a beneficent landlord; and his first
care was to build good cottages for all the
labouring men on his estates. He had
entered into minute calculations as to the
amount of illness which might be prevented
amongst the poorer classes by a careful
selection of the materials to be used in the
building of their dwellings. In a word, he
was tender, thoughtful, and anxious in his

The Prince's care for the labouring classes.

efforts for the welfare of the labouring
man. His constancy of purpose in that,
as in other things, was worthy of all
imitation. He did not become tired of
benevolence. It was not the fancy of a
day for him. It was the sustained purpose of a life.

The Prince's love of Art must be spoken *What he*
of separately, for it was something peculiar *sought for
in Art.*
to himself. He saw through Art into what,
in its highest form, it expressed—the beautiful. He cared not so much for a close
representation of the things of daily life,
as for that ideal world which Art shadows
forth, and interprets to mankind. Hence
his love for many a picture which might
not be a masterpiece of drawing or of
colouring, but which had tenderness and
reverence in it, and told of something that
was remote from common life, and high
and holy.

Joined with this longing for an interpre-
tation of the ideal, there was in the Prince
a love of Art for itself—a pleasure in the
skilful execution of a design, whether exe-
cuted by himself or others. He was no

mean artist, and his knowledge of Art
stretched forth into various directions. But
this was not the remarkable point. There
have been other Princes who have been
artists. It was in his love of Art—in his
keen perception of what Art could do, and
of what was its highest province—that he
excelled many men who were distinguished
artists themselves, and had given their lives
to the cultivation of Art.

Skill in or-
ganization.

Again, there was the Prince's skill in
organization, that almost amounted to an
art, which he showed in all the work he
touched, and in everything he advised upon.

It may, therefore, justly be said that the
Prince approached the highest realms of
Art in various ways, which are seldom
combined in any one person : in his fondness for what is romantic and ideal, in his
love of skill and handicraft, and in his
uniform desire for masterly organization.

What the
Prince did for
agriculture.

In distinguishing the various branches of
Art which the Prince devoted himself to,
and loved to further, Agriculture must be
particularly mentioned, not only on account
of the great interest he took in it, and of

the practical skill he brought to it, but because of the felicitous results which followed
upon his enterprises in this department.
As regards works of High Art, it is not
much that the wisest Prince, or the most
judicious patron, can do to further them.
They depend upon the existence, at any particular period, of men or women of genius;
and the production of such works lies in
a region which is beyond and above the
patronage even of the most judicious patrons.
But it is not so with Agriculture; and the
Prince might fairly lay claim to having
himself done much towards that improvement in agriculture which, happily for this
country, has been so marked and so rapid
within the last twenty years. Men are
always much influenced by what their supe-
riors in station do. And that the Prince
should have been one of the first persons
in this country to appreciate the merits of
Deep Drainage, to employ Steam Power in
cultivation (a power which does not require
to be fed when it is put by in its stable
after the day's work), and to apply the
resources of Chemistry to Practical Agriculture, ensured the welcome consequence

that there would be many followers where
the foremost man of England was anxious
and ready to lead the way. That, with a
large breadth of the lands of Great Britain
partially tilled, or scarcely cultivated at all,
the British Nation should not unfrequently
have to expend twenty or thirty millions of
money in foreign corn, is a reproach against
our practical sagacity, in which the Prince
at least can have no share of the blame.

It has been said that, if we knew any
man's life intimately, there would be some
great and peculiar moral to be derived from
it—some tendency to be noted, which other
men, observing it in his career, might seek
to correct in themselves. I cannot help
thinking that I see what may be the moral
to be derived from a study of the Prince's

The Prince
too much
interested in
too many
things.

life. It is one which applies only to a
few amongst the highest natures; and,
simply stated, it is this—that he cared too
much about too many things.

His craving
for perfection.

Moreover, everything in which he was
concerned must be done supremely well if
it was to please and satisfy him. The great
German, Goethe, had the same defect, or

rather the same superabundance. He would take inordinate pains even in writing a short note, that it should be admirably written. He did not understand the merit of second-best; but everything that was to be done must be done perfectly. It was thus with the Prince. In the choice of a jewel, in the placing of a statue, in the laying out of a walk, in the direction of a party of pleasure, his reasoning mind must be satisfied; and he longed that everything that was to be, should be the best of its kind.

Now men of this nature, with an abiding aspiration towards what is beautiful, and such an inordinate appreciation of what is reasonable, require also to have an extraordinary stock of health,* otherwise they make extravagant demands upon their powers of thought and attention, and thus upon the primary elements of life.

Strain upon the health.

---

* And the Prince had very good health. At any rate he had begun with a fine constitution. Every one of the chief organs of life was well developed in him, with the exception of a heart that was not quite equal to the work put upon it; so that he mostly had but a feeble pulse. It was upon the nervous energy that this constant stress of work, and this striving after excellence in everything, must have told, as such demands do tell upon all men of that high nature.

The man who insists upon having a good reason for everything he thinks and does, has set himself a task which it requires almost superhuman energy to master. With a boundless appetite for knowledge, the Prince declined to be superficial in anything; and whatever question was brought to him, he set to work at it with a resolution to give his best attention to solve it. All men, when they find such a mind to lean upon, delight to bring their difficulties to it; and in the Prince's case his extraordinary good nature and prompt sympathy forbade him to ignore any question which interested his fellow-men. I cannot help thinking that, but for this peculiarity in his nature—a peculiarity which, regret it as we may, we cannot but love and admire—he would have lived for many years longer, to be, as he had always been, the worthiest and ablest supporter of the Throne, and the foremost advocate of all that held out a promise of increasing the welfare of the people.

It may here be well to remind the reader that the Prince was only forty-two years of age when he died; and that the sagacity and prudence for which he gained a just renown, were manifested at an age when many other men, even of the brightest sort, are far from showing maturity of judgment. This early death, too, makes the great amount of knowledge that he had acquired all the more extraordinary. And, altogether, we may say that seldom has there been compressed into a life more of thought, energy, and anxious care, than was crowded into his. His death appears especially premature at a period when we are accustomed to have great soldiers, lawyers, and statesmen distinguishing themselves, and almost showing new faculties, after they have reached the threescore years and ten so pathetically spoken of by the Psalmist. If the Prince had lived to attain what we now think a good old age, he would inevitably have become the most accomplished statesman and the most guiding personage in Europe—a man to whose arbitrement fierce national quarrels might have been submitted, and by whose influence calamitous wars might have been averted.

So subtly are men constituted, and so difficult is it, even from a careful enume-

ration of their qualities, to get at the result
of their nature, and to understand the men
themselves, that it would be possible, notwithstanding all that has been justly said
in praise of the Prince, that he might still
have failed to be a very loveable character.
You meet with people against whom nothing
in dispraise can well be urged, and for whom
high-sounding panegyrics might justly be
written, who yet are not pleasant, amiable,
or loveable. It was not so, however, with
the Prince. The mere enumeration of his
high qualities and his good tendencies would
fail to give a just representation of his
peculiarly gentle, tender, and pathetic cast
of mind. Indeed this kind of character is
rather German than English, and had
always been much noted as a prevailing
character in the Prince's family. Though
eminently practical, and therefore suited to
the people he came to dwell amongst, he
had in a high degree that gentleness, that
softness, and that romantic nature, which
belong to his race and his nation, and which
make them very pleasant to live with, and
very tender in all their social and family
relations.

The gentle-
ness of the
Prince.

Finally there was in the Prince a quality which I think may be noticed as belonging to most men of genius and of mark. I mean a certain childlike simplicity. It is noticed of such men that, mentally speaking, they do not grow old like other men. There is always a playfulness about them, a certain innocency of character, and a power of taking interest in what surrounds them, which we naturally associate with the beauty of youthfulness. It is a pity to use a foreign word if one can help it, but it illustrates the character of such men to say that they never can become "*blasés.*" Those who had the good fortune to know the Prince, will, I am sure, admit the truth of this remark as applied to him; and will agree in the opinion that neither disaster, sickness, nor any other form of human adversity, would have been able to harden his receptive nature, or deaden his soul to the wide-spread interests of humanity. He would always have been young in heart; and a great proof of this was his singular attractiveness to all those about him who were young.

One gift that the Prince possessed, which

The abiding youthfulness of men of genius possessed by him.

tended to make him a favourite with the
young, was his peculiar aptitude for im-
parting knowledge. Indeed, the skill he
showed in explaining anything, whether
addressed to the young or the old, ensured
the readiest attention ; and it would not be
easy to find, even among the first Pro-
fessors and Teachers of this age, any one
who could surpass the Prince in giving, in
the fewest words, and with the least use
of technical terms, a lucid account of some
difficult matter in science which he had
mastered—mastered not only for himself,
but for all others who had the advantage of
listening to him.

The one of his children who was most
capable of judging of what his conduct had
been to all his children as a father and a
friend, speaks thus of him :—

" But in no relation of life did the
" goodness and greatness of his character
" appear more than in the management
" of his children. The most judicious,
" impartial, and loving of fathers, he was
" at once the friend and master, ever by
" his example enforcing the precepts he
" sought to instil."

The Prince's marriage was singularly felicitous. The tastes, the aims, the hopes, the aspirations of the Royal Pair were the same. Their mutual respect and confidence went on increasing. Their affection grew, if possible, even warmer and more intense as the years of their married life advanced. Companions in their domestic employments, in their daily labours for the State, and, indeed, in almost every occupation,—the burthens and the difficulties of life were thus lessened more than by half for each one of the persons thus happily united in this true marriage of the soul. When the fatal blow was struck, and the Prince was removed from this world, it is difficult to conceive a position of greater sorrow, and one, indeed, more utterly forlorn, than that which became the lot of the Survivor— deprived of him whom She Herself has described as being the " Life of Her Life."

To follow out his wishes—to realize his hopes — to conduct his enterprizes to a happy issue—to make his loss as little felt as possible by a sorrowing country and fatherless children :—these are the objects which, since his death, it has been the chief aim and intent of Her Majesty to accomplish. That strength may be given her to fulfil these high purposes, is the constant prayer of her subjects, who have not ceased, from the first moment of her bereavement, to feel the tenderest sympathy for her; and who, giving a reality to that which in the case of most Sovereigns is but a phrase, have thus shown that the Queen is indeed, in their hearts, the Mother of her people.

How the Prince was mourned for.

It is a matter of history that, at the untimely end of the Prince, the sorrow of the whole nation went with him to his grave. That was due to his great public qualities: but, within a narrower circle, the endearing qualities of his nature called forth a deeper anguish and a more abiding affliction. Never was there a man more mourned by his family, by his friends, by those of his household, and by all persons who had come into contact or connection with him. This is perhaps the most favourable trait, the most undeniable proof of goodness and of greatness of heart, that can be brought forward of any man ; for though we read upon tombstones of the undying regret of family and friends, it is in reality given to few amongst the sons of men to leave a blank in the lives of many other persons, which refuses to be filled up—a fond and passionate regret which may be soothed, but which, in their devoted hearts, can never be effaced.

NOTE.

IT must be obvious to the reader of this Introduction that the writer has received the most valuable and important aid from those who, by their constant intercourse with the Prince Consort, could best appreciate the high qualities which shone forth in his domestic life—from persons in the Royal Household who saw him daily—from Members of the Royal Family—and especially from the Queen Herself. To Her Majesty the writer is indebted for a view of the Prince's character in which a loving and profound appreciation is combined with the most earnest desire for exact truth and faithfulness. There is not any one who could have been cognizant of all the various traits of the Prince enumerated in this Introduction, unless he had been instructed by Her, who alone saw, with the full light of a complete affection, into the whole beauty and merit of the character of this remarkable Man.

LONDON,
    October, 1862.

THE OFFICE

COMMANDER-IN-CHIEF.

THE foregoing is simply an Introduction to the Prince Consort's Speeches, with some outlines of the Prince's character. It is in no respect meant to anticipate the publication of his Life; and, consequently, no documents have been inserted, or even alluded to, which would be required for the illustration of that life.

One exception, however, to this rule the Queen has graciously consented to make. Amongst the manuscripts left by the Prince, there is a memorandum in his own handwriting on a subject of great importance in itself. But now, alas! the memorandum is of more importance still, as illustrating, in a remarkable manner, the Prince's character and conduct. In this document he clearly defines his own position, and lays out as it were the main scheme and purpose of his life. His words on this occasion are like a lamp raised up high on a vessel,

F

which casts long lines of light upon the waves
before and after, showing the course which has
been passed over, and that which will be passed
over, as the ship speeds right onwards through
the dark waters of the uncertain sea.

In the Introduction a character has been drawn,
which might be cavilled at from its having so
much that is bright in it, and so little that
affords any contrast whatever of darkness. The
Prince is there depicted as a most self-denying
man. Those who lived with him knew that it
was so; they knew that the habit of self-denial
pervaded his whole life. But it might be difficult for the rest of the world to be assured of
the full extent of this self-denial.

After reading the document in question,
there will no longer be any doubt upon this
point. It can hardly be imagined that anything could be more tempting to a young
man, placed as the Prince was, than to have
almost within his grasp such a grand and
distinct position as that of the Commander-in-
Chief of the British Army. Throughout the
memorandum it is evident that the Prince felt
the temptation deeply while he abjured it. It
was not the cold refusal of a person indifferent

to what was offered to him; but it was the stern self-sacrifice of one who, abounding in noble ambition, would dearly like to take the honour and the labour which he feels it his duty to decline.

The circumstances portrayed in the memorandum are very dramatic, and are exceedingly interesting, if only on that account. We cannot but picture to ourselves the tender wife already but too justly anxious for her Consort's health; the aged Duke, with his well-known and long-tried devotion to the Throne, urging, in his decided manner, upon the Prince the acceptance of this much-coveted post; and the Prince modestly and decisively putting it from him as a thing he must not have. There was wisdom in the motives which led the old warrior and statesman to make the proposal. But there was a higher wisdom in those of the young Prince who steadily refused to entertain the offer: a wisdom not proceeding from a nice perception of what was safe for self-interest, or from a skilful balancing of consequences, but from an instinct of goodness cultivated by chivalry into the highest self-devotion.

The resolution which the Prince announces in this memorandum — to sink his own individual existence in that of the Queen—had long been acted upon by him even then, and was never afterwards departed from. It was not repented of: it gave a colour to his whole career : it sustained him in long days of wearisome, commonplace labour : it became a part of his being; and he never surrendered it but with his last breath.

Many a reader of the foregoing Introduction, not having met with anything like the Prince's character in ordinary life, might naturally imagine it to have been drawn by too partial a hand. But this thought will vanish, when he sees the Prince unconsciously depicted by himself, and thus learns, from undoubted authority, what was the object, what the meaning, and what the settled purpose of his well-spent life.

In allowing this Memorandum of the Prince to be published, the Queen is also actuated by another motive in addition to those which have already been mentioned. It affords Her Majesty a fitting opportunity for expressing, in the most clear and ample manner, that which for many years she has desired to express. During the Prince's life, the Queen often longed to make known to the world the ever-present, watchful, faithful, invaluable aid which she received from the Prince Consort in the conduct of the public business. Her Majesty could hardly endure even then to be silent on this subject, and not to declare how much her Reign owed to him. And now the Queen can no longer refrain from uttering what she has so long felt, and from proclaiming the irreparable loss to the public service, as well as to herself and to her family, which the Prince's death has occasioned.

The position of Her Majesty, for many years accustomed to this loving aid, and now suddenly bereft of it, can with difficulty be imagined to the full extent of its heaviness and its sadness. Desolate and sombre, as the Queen most deeply feels, lies the way before her ;—a path, however, of duty and of labour, which, relying on the loyal attachment and sympathy of her people, she will, with God's blessing, strive to pursue ; but where she fears her faltering steps will often show they lack the tender and affectionate support which, on all occasions, Her Majesty was wont to receive from her beloved husband, the Prince.

The circumstances which preceded the drawing up of this Memorandum by the Prince, are as follows :—

On the death of Sir J. Macdonald, the Adjutant-General, in March, 1850, a suggestion was made to amalgamate the two offices of Adjutant and Quartermaster-General under a single head, to be called Chief of the Staff. The Duke of Wellington was in consequence summoned to Windsor, and several conversations ensued, in the course of which the Duke proposed that arrangements should be made with a view to the Prince's ultimately succeeding himself as Commander-in-Chief.*

The following are extracts from the minutes made by the Prince of those conversations, as far as they related to that proposal :—

Windsor Castle, April 3, 1850.

I went yesterday to see the Duke of Wellington in his room after his arrival at the Castle,

---

* The circumstances narrated above, and the conduct of the Prince Consort upon them, were related by Earl Russell very succinctly and accurately in his speech in the House of Commons, Jan. 31, 1854.

our conversation soon turning to the question of
the vacant Adjutant-Generalship. I asked the
Duke what he was prepared to recommend.
He said he had had a letter on the subject
recommending the union of the two offices of
Adjutant-General and Quartermaster-General,
and he placed his answer to it in my hands.
He then proceeded to say that he thought it
necessary that we should cast our eyes a little
before us. He was past 80 years, and would
next month enter upon his 82nd. He was, thank
God! very well and strong, and ready to do
anything; but he could not last for ever, and in
the natural course of events we must look to
a change ere long. As long as he was there, he
did the duty of all the offices himself. . . . . To
form a new office by uniting the duties of Adjutant-General and Quartermaster-General in the
person of a Chief of the Staff, as was the practice
in some foreign armies, would be to appoint two
different persons to do the same duty, which
would never answer. The Chief of the Staff
would again have to subdivide his office into an
Adjutant-General and Quartermaster-General's
Department, and nothing would be gained.

However, the Duke saw the greatest advantage in having a Chief of the Staff, if, after his death, that arrangement should be made which he had always looked to, and which he considered the best, viz. *that I should assume the command of the army.*

He was sure I could not do it without such a Chief of the Staff, who would be responsible before the public, and carry on the official communications with the other Government Departments. For this contingency he was prepared to organize the machinery now, and he would answer for its success. . . . .

I answered to the Duke that I should be very slow to make up my mind to undertake so great a responsibility — that I was not sure of my fitness for it, on account of my want of military experience, &c. (to which the Duke replied, that with good honest intentions one could do a great deal, and that he should not be the least afraid on that score) — whether I could perform the duties consistently with my other avocations, as I should not like to undertake what I could not carry through, not knowing what time or attention they would require.

The Duke answered, that it would certainly require both time and attention, for nothing could be done without my knowledge, or without my order, but that the detail would be worked out by the Chief of the Staff. He had thoroughly considered that, and would make it work. . . . He always stood up for the principle of the army being commanded by the Sovereign ; and he endeavoured to make the practice agree with that theory, by scrupulously taking, on every point, the Queen's pleasure before he acted. But, were he gone, he saw no security, unless I undertook the command myself, and thus supplied what was deficient in the constitutional working of the theory, arising from the circumstance of the present Sovereign being a lady. Strictly constitutionally I should certainly be responsible for my acts, but before the world in general the Chief of the Staff would bear the responsibility, and for that office the man of the greatest name and weight in the army ought to be selected. He repeated that he thought this the most desirable arrangement, and would at once work it out to the best of his ability. . . . I begged him to leave me time to consider the proposal.

In the evening the Queen gave the Duke of
Wellington an audience, I being present. After
having set out by saying he was most anxious
to let the Queen know and feel all he knew
and felt about it—in fact, to *think aloud*—the
Duke repeated what he had said to me in the
morning, and we discussed the question further.
I said that there were several points which still
required to be considered. . . . The offer was
so tempting for a young man, that I felt bound
to look most closely to all the objections to it, in
order to come to a right decision. . . . The
Queen, as a lady, was not able at all times to
perform the many duties imposed upon her ;
moreover she had no Private Secretary who
worked for her, as former Sovereigns had had.
The only person who helped her, and who could
assist her, in the multiplicity of work which
ought to be done by the Sovereign, was myself.
I should be very sorry to undertake any duty
which would absorb my time and attention so
much for *one* Department, as to interfere with
my general usefulness to the Queen. . . . The
Queen added, that I already worked harder than
she liked to see, and than she thought was good

for my health,* which I did not allow—answering, that, on the contrary, business must naturally increase with time, and ought to increase, if the Sovereign's duties to the country were to be thoroughly performed; but that I was anxious no more should fall upon her than could be helped.

The Duke seemed struck with this consideration, and said he had not overlooked it, but might not have given it all the weight it deserved, and that he would reflect further upon it.

We agreed at last that this question could not be satisfactorily solved unless we knew the exact

---

* The anxiety of the Queen lest the Prince should injure his health by his excessive attention to public business, naturally continued to increase.

In 1860, when the Society of Arts renewed the proposal for holding a second International Exhibition, the Queen wrote to Lord Granville, without the knowledge of the Prince, expressing Her earnest hope that he (Lord Granville) would do all that in him lay to prevent the responsibility and labour of conducting the undertaking being thrown in any way on His Royal Highness.

The Queen felt deeply the necessity for averting any addition to the heavy work already entailed on the Prince by the assistance and support (every day more needful to Her) which he gave Her in the transaction of all public business; and Her Majesty was convinced that he could not again undertake the labour he had gone through in conducting the first Exhibition to its successful termination, without injury to that health which was not only most precious to Herself and his family, but to the country, and even to the world.

duties which had to be performed ; and the Queen charged the Duke to draw up a memorandum in which these should be detailed, and his general opinion explained, so that we might found a decision on that paper. This the Duke promised to do.

Windsor Castle, April 6, 1850.

After a good deal of reflection on the Duke of Wellington's proposal, I went to pay him a visit yesterday morning in his room, and found him prepared with his memorandum, which he handed to me. After having read it, I said to him that I must consider my position as a whole, which was that of the consort and confidential adviser and assistant of a female sovereign. Her interest and good should stand foremost, and all other considerations must be viewed in reference to this, and in subordination to it. The question then was simply, whether I should not weaken my means of attending to all parts of the constitutional position alike—political, social, and moral—if I devoted myself to a special branch, however important that might be ; and that I was afraid this would be the consequence

of my becoming Commander-in-Chief. It was quite true that the Sovereign being a lady naturally weakened her relation to the army, and that the duty rested upon me of supplying that deficiency, and would do so still more when the protection which the Duke afforded to the Crown should be unfortunately withdrawn. But I doubted whether this might not be accomplished without my becoming especially responsible for the command of the army. There was no branch of public business in which I was not now supporting the Queen, &c. &c. . . . .
The Duke replied he quite saw that my position ought to be looked at as a whole. He felt the extreme difficulty and delicacy of it, and was kind enough to add that he approved of, and the public did full justice to the way in which I had hitherto maintained it. I begged him to leave me a little time for consideration, that I wanted to study his memorandum, and would finally write to him upon the subject.

Two days afterwards the Prince wrote to the Duke a letter, of which the following are extracts :—

My dear Duke,

The Queen and myself have thoroughly considered your proposal to join the offices of Adjutant-General and Quartermaster-General into one of a Chief of the Staff, with a view to facilitate the future assumption of the command of the army by myself. . . . . The question whether it will be advisable that I should take the command of the army or not, has been most anxiously weighed by me, and I have come to the conclusion that my decision ought entirely and solely to be guided by the consideration, whether it would interfere with, or assist, my position of Consort of the Sovereign, and the performance of the duties which this position imposes upon me.

This position is a most peculiar and delicate one. Whilst a female sovereign has a great many disadvantages in comparison with a king, yet, if she is married, and her husband understands and does his duty, her position, on the other hand, has many compensating advantages, and, in the long run, will be found even to be stronger than that of a male sovereign. But

this requires that the husband should entirely
sink his *own individual* existence in that of his
wife—that he should aim at no power by himself
or for himself—should shun all ostentation—assume no separate responsibility before the public
—but make his position entirely a part of hers—
fill up every gap which, as a woman, she would
naturally leave in the exercise of her regal
functions — continually and anxiously watch
every part of the public business, in order to be
able to advise and assist her at any moment, in
any of the multifarious and difficult questions
or duties brought before her, sometimes international, sometimes political, or social, or personal.
As the natural head of her family, superinten-
dent of her household, manager of her private
affairs, sole *confidential* adviser in politics, and
only assistant in her communications with the
officers of the government, he is besides the
husband of the Queen, the tutor of the Royal
children, the private secretary of the Sovereign,
and her permanent minister.

How far would it be consistent with this
position to undertake the management and
administration of a most important branch of

the public service, and the individual responsibility attaching to it—becoming an Executive
Officer of the Crown, receiving the Queen's
commands through her Secretaries of State,
&c. &c.? I feel sure that, having undertaken
the responsibility, I should not be satisfied to
leave the business and real work in the hands of
another (the Chief of the Staff), but should feel
it my duty to look to them myself. But whilst
I should in this manner perform duties which, I
am sure, every able General Officer, who has
gained experience in the field, would be able to
perform better than myself, who have not had
the advantage of such experience, most important duties connected with the welfare of the
Sovereign would be left unperformed, which
nobody *could* perform but myself. I am afraid,
therefore, that I must discard the tempting
idea of being placed in command of the British
Army.

SPEECHES

OF

HIS ROYAL HIGHNESS

THE

PRINCE CONSORT.

CONTENTS.

SPEECHES.

AT A MEETING FOR THE ABOLITION OF SLAVERY.

[JUNE 1st, 1840.]

I HAVE been induced to preside at the Meeting of this Society, from a conviction of its paramount importance to the great interests of humanity and justice.

I deeply regret that the benevolent and persevering exertions of England to abolish that atrocious traffic in human beings (at once the desolation of Africa and the blackest stain upon civilized Europe) have not as yet led to any satisfactory conclusion. But I sincerely trust that this great country will not relax in its efforts until it has finally, and for ever, put an end to a state of things so repugnant to the spirit of Christianity, and the best feelings of our nature.

Let us therefore trust that Providence will prosper our exertions in so holy a cause, and that (under the auspices of our Queen and Her Government) we may at no distant period be rewarded by the accomplishment of the great and humane object for the promotion of which we have this day met.

LITERARY FUND, 1842.

1.

I PROPOSE the health of the Queen, who highly appreciates the tendency of this Institution, and sincerely interests herself in its welfare.

" THE QUEEN, OUR MUNIFICENT PATRON."

2.

I return you my warmest thanks for the great kindness with which you have received this toast. It will always be most gratifying to my feelings to contribute in the smallest degree towards the welfare of any of the excellent Institutions which so prominently distinguish this country.

3.

The toast which I have now to propose to you is the Prosperity of this Institution.

It stands unrivalled in any country, and ought to command our warmest sympathies, as providing for the exigencies of those who, following the call of Genius, and forgetting every other consideration, pursue merely the cultivation of the human mind and science. What can then be more proper for us than gratefully to remember the benefits derived from their disinterested exertions, and cheerfully to contribute to their wants?

I conclude with the ardent wish that the object for which we have this day met will be answered in the most ample and generous way.

" Prosperity to this Institution."

4.

I am sure you will all gladly join me in drinking the health of our worthy President the Marquis of Lansdowne. He would not wish me to enumerate his merits as a patron of the Arts and Science, so well known to this assembly; but it is a satisfaction to me to have an opportunity of expressing how much I esteem them.

" OUR PRESIDENT."

THE CORPORATION OF TRINITY HOUSE.

WITH much sincerity I return you my best thanks for the toast which has just been drunk.

I feel a pride in the cause which makes me a guest this day with the Corporation of the Trinity House, to whose exertions in the discharge of your important duties this great country is so deeply indebted.

That these exertions, upon which not only the good of the Mercantile Marine depends, but which have so essentially contributed to the welfare of the Navy, may in their various and important branches be always crowned with success, I warmly wish; and I cannot refrain from expressing how happy I should feel if by my admission into your Corporation I should ever be afforded the smallest opportunity of forwarding any of your objects.

The distinguished honour conferred upon me this day, an honour aspired to and prized by eminent men of every age, will always be held in my most lively remembrance.

[When the heart flies out before the understanding, it saves the judgment a world of pains.]

AT THE MEETING OF THE

SOCIETY FOR IMPROVING THE CONDITION
OF THE LABOURING CLASSES.

[MAY 18TH, 1848.]

LADIES AND GENTLEMEN,—

WHEN four years since this Society for the Improvement of the Condition of the Labouring Classes was first established on its present footing, I accepted with great pleasure the offer of becoming its President.

I saw in this offer a proof of your appreciation of my feelings of sympathy and interest for that class of our community which has most of the toil, and least of the enjoyments, of this world. I conceived that great advantage would accrue from the endeavours of influential persons, who were wholly disinterested, to act the part of a friend to those who required that advice and assistance which none but a friend could tender with advantage.

This Society has always held this object before

its eyes, and has been labouring in that direction.
You are all aware that it has established model
lodging-houses, loan-funds, and the system of
allotments of ground in different parts of the
country ; but it has been careful only to establish
examples and models, mindful that any real improvement which was to take place must be the
result of the exertions of the working people
themselves.

I have just come from the model lodging-
house, the opening of which we celebrate this
day ; and I feel convinced that its existence will,
by degrees, cause a complete change in the
domestic comforts of the labouring classes, as it
will exhibit to them, that with real economy can
be combined advantages with which few of them
have hitherto been acquainted ; whilst it will
show to those who possess capital to invest, that
they may do so with great profit and advantage
to themselves, at the same time that they are
dispensing those comforts to which I have
alluded, to their poorer brethren.

Depend upon it, the interests of classes too
often contrasted are identical, and it is only
ignorance which prevents their uniting for each
other's advantage. To dispel that ignorance, to
show how man can help man, notwithstanding

the complicated state of civilized society, ought
to be the aim of every philanthropic person ; but
it is more peculiarly the duty of those who,
under the blessing of Divine Providence, enjoy
station, wealth, and education.

Let them be careful, however, to avoid any
dictatorial interference with labour and employment, which frightens away capital, destroys that
freedom of thought and independence of action
which must remain to every one if he is to work
out his own happiness, and impairs that confidence under which alone engagements for
mutual benefit are possible.

God has created man imperfect, and left him
with many wants, as it were to stimulate each to
individual exertion, and to make all feel that it
is only by united exertions and combined action
that these imperfections can be supplied, and
these wants satisfied.   This presupposes self-
reliance and confidence in each other.   To show
the way how these individual exertions can be
directed with the greatest benefit, and to foster
that confidence upon which the readiness to
assist each other depends, this Society deems its
most sacred duty.

There has been no ostentatious display of
charity or munificence, nor the pretension of

becoming the arbiter of the fate of thousands, but the quiet working out of particular schemes of social improvement; for which, however, as I said before, the Society has only established examples for the community at large to follow.

The report of the proceedings of last year will now be laid before you.

I must say—I hope I may say—that the Society has proceeded satisfactorily towards the accomplishment of its objects; and that is owing particularly to the kind feelings, the great experience, and undoubted zeal of Lord Ashley.

The next step which we contemplate taking is the erection of a model lodging-house for families. I have no doubt that the meeting will enable us to carry out that step, and that the attention of the public will be more generally directed to the objects which we have in view.

AT THE MEETING OF

THE ROYAL AGRICULTURAL SOCIETY.

[HELD AT YORK, JULY 13TH, 1848.]

GENTLEMEN,—

I HAVE to thank you most sincerely for your having drunk my health with so much cordiality. It has been a great satisfaction to me to have been able this year to pay an old debt in appearing at this interesting and useful meeting.

All I have seen to-day exhibits a bright picture of the progress of British agriculture, and for much of this progress the country is indebted to this Society.

Agriculture, which was once the main pursuit of this as of every other nation, holds even now, notwithstanding the development of commerce and manufactures, a fundamental position in the realm; and although time has changed the position which the owner of the land, with his feudal dependants, held in the empire, the country gentleman with his wife and children, the country clergyman, the tenant, and the labourer, still

H

form a great, and I hope united, family, in which we gladly recognize the foundation of our social state.

Science and mechanical improvement have in these days changed the mere practice of cultivating the soil into an industrial pursuit, requiring capital, machinery, industry, and skill, and perseverance in the struggle of competition. This is another great change, but we must consider it a great *progress*, as it demands higher efforts and a higher intelligence.

Conscious of these changes, we Agriculturists of England assemble together in this annual meeting of the Royal Agricultural Society, in order to communicate to each other our various experiences, to exhibit the progress that some may have made in the applications of science, and others in the adaptation of machinery, or in the successful rearing of animals.

Feeling, as I do, a great interest in these noble pursuits and their paramount importance, and having myself experienced the pleasures and the little pangs attending them, I feel highly gratified that it should have been confided to me to propose to you the toast of the day, " Success to " the Royal Agricultural Society of England;" and I trust that you will heartily respond to it.

AT THE LAYING THE FIRST STONE

OF THE

GREAT GRIMSBY DOCKS.

[APRIL 18TH, 1849.]

My Lord,*—

I THANK you most sincerely for the kind terms in which you have proposed my health, and you, gentlemen, for the cordial manner in which you have received it.

The act which has this day been performed, and in which you were kind enough to desire that I should take the chief part, could not but make a deep impression upon me.

We have been laying the foundation not only of a Dock, as a place of refuge, safety, and refitment for mercantile shipping, and calculated even to receive the largest steamers in Her Majesty's Navy, but it may be, and I hope it will be, the foundation of a great commercial port, destined in after times, when we shall long have quitted this scene, and when our names even may be forgotten, to form another centre of life to the

* The late Earl of Yarborough, Lord Lieutenant of the county of Lincoln.

vast and ever-increasing commerce of the world,
and an important link in the connection of the
East and the West. Nay, if I contemplate the
extraordinary rapidity of development which cha-
racterizes the undertakings of this age, it may not
even be too much to expect that some of us may
live yet to see this prospect in part realized.

This work has been undertaken, like almost
all the national enterprises of this great country,
by *private* exertion, with *private* capital, and at
private risk; and it shares with them likewise
that other feature so peculiar to the enterprises
of Englishmen, that, strongly attached as they
are to the institutions of their country, and
gratefully acknowledging the protection of those
laws under which their enterprises are undertaken and flourish, they love to connect them, in
some manner, directly with the authority of the
Crown and the person of their Sovereign; and
it is the appreciation of this circumstance which
has impelled me at once to respond to your call,
as the readiest mode of testifying to you how
strongly Her Majesty the Queen values and re-
ciprocates this feeling.

I have derived an additional gratification from
this visit, as it has brought me for the first time
to the county of Lincoln, so celebrated for its

agricultural pursuits, and showing a fine example
of the energy of the national character, which
has, by dint of perseverance, succeeded in trans-
forming unhealthy swamps into the richest and
most fertile soil in the kingdom. I could not
have witnessed finer specimens of Lincolnshire
farming than have been shown to me on his
estates by your Chairman, my noble host, who
has made me acquainted, not only with the
agricultural improvements which are going on
amongst you, but with that most gratifying state
of the relation between Landlord and Tenant
which exists here, and which I hope may become
an example, in time to be followed throughout
the country. Here it is that the real advantage
and the prosperity of both do not depend upon
the written letter of agreements, but on that
mutual trust and confidence which has in this
country for a long time been held a sufficient
security to both, to warrant the extensive outlay of capital, and the engagement in farming
operations on the largest scale.

Let me, in conclusion, propose to you as a
toast, " Prosperity to the Great Grimsby Docks;"
and let us invoke the Almighty to bestow His
blessing on this work, under which alone it can
prosper.

AT THE PUBLIC MEETING OF THE

SERVANTS' PROVIDENT AND BENEVOLENT
SOCIETY.

[MAY 16TH, 1849.]

GENTLEMEN,—

THE object for which we have assembled here
to-day is not one of charity, but of friendly
advice and assistance to be tendered to a large
and important class of our fellow-countrymen.

Who would not feel the deepest interest in the
welfare of their Domestic Servants ? Whose
heart would fail to sympathize with those who
minister to us in all the wants of daily life, attend
us in sickness, receive us upon our first appearance in this world, and even extend their cares
to our mortal remains, who live under our roof,
form our household, and are a part of our
family ?

And yet upon inquiry we find that in this
metropolis the greater part of the inmates of the
workhouse are domestic servants.

I am sure that this startling fact is no proof

either of a want of kindness and liberality in masters towards their servants, or of vice in the latter, but is the natural consequence of that peculiar position in which the domestic servant is placed, passing periods during his life in which he shares in the luxuries of an opulent master, and others in which he has not even the means of earning sufficient to sustain him through the day.

It is the consideration of these peculiar vicissitudes which makes it the duty of both masters and servants to endeavour to discover and to agree upon some means for carrying the servant through life, safe from the temptations of the prosperous, and from the sufferings of the evil day. It is on that account that I rejoice at this meeting, and have gladly consented to take the chair at it, to further the objects of the " Servants' " Provident and Benevolent Society."

I conceive that this Society is founded upon a right principle, as it follows out the dictates of a correct appreciation of human nature, which requires every man, by personal exertion, and according to his own choice, to work out his own happiness ; which prevents his valuing, nay, even his feeling satisfaction at, the prosperity which others have made for him. It is founded upon a right principle, because it endeavours to trace out a plan according to which, by providence, by present self-denial and perseverance, not only will the servant be raised in his physical and moral condition, but the master also will be taught how to direct his efforts in aiding the servant in his labour to secure to himself resources in cases of sickness, old age, and want of employment. It is founded on a right principle, because in its financial scheme there is no temptation held out to the servant by the prospect of possible extravagant advantages, which tend to transform his providence into a species of gambling; by convivial meetings, which lead him to ulterior expense; or by the privilege of balloting for the few prizes, which draws him into all the waste of time and excitement of an electioneering contest.

Such are the characteristics of several institutions, upon which servants and many of our other industrial classes place their reliance. And what can be more heartrending than to witness the breaking of banks, and the failure of such institutions, which not only mar the prospects of these unhappy people, and plunge them into sudden destitution, but destroy in others all confidence in the honesty or sagacity of those who preach to them the advantages of providence?

Let them well consider that, if they must embark in financial speculations, if they like to have convivial meetings, if they claim the right of governing the concerns of their own body, they must not risk for this, in one stake, their whole future existence, the whole prosperity of their families. Let them always bear in mind, that their savings are capital, that capital will only return a certain interest, and that any advantage offered beyond that interest has to be purchased at a commensurate risk of the capital itself.

The financial advantages which this Society holds out to servants rest upon the credit of the country at large, upon the faith of the Government, and are regulated by an Act of Parliament, called " the Deferred Annuities Act." They are shortly these : " According to published tables, " which I have before me, persons, whose fixed " income is below 150*l.* per annum, can, by small " instalments, purchase annuities deferred not less " than ten years, but beyond that limit to com- " mence at any period the depositor may name. " One annuity cannot be more than 30*l.*, but he " may purchase distinct annuities for his wife, or

"for his children on having attained to their
"fifteenth year. Should he at any time wish to
"withdraw his deposits before the annuity has
"commenced, they will be returned to him;
"should he die before that period, the deposits
"will be returned to the heirs. In such cases
"the only loss will be the interest upon the
"money deposited."

Although this wise and benevolent measure
has been enacted so long ago as the third year
of the reign of King William IV., I find, to my
deep regret, that, during that whole time, only
about 600 persons have availed themselves of its
provisions. I can discover no other reason for
this inadequate success, but that the existence of
the Act is not generally known, or that people
are afraid of law and Acts of Parliament, which
they cannot understand on account of their
complicated technical wording. I have heard
another reason stated, to which, however, I give
little credit, namely, that servants fear lest a
knowledge that they are able to purchase annuities by savings from their wages might induce
their masters to reduce them. I have a better
opinion of the disposition of employers generally,
and am convinced that, on the contrary, nothing
counteracts more the liberality of masters than

the idea, not wholly unfounded, that an increase of means, instead of prompting to saving, leads to extravagance.

It is one of the main objects of this meeting to draw public attention to this " Deferred Annuities " Act," and the main object of this Society is to form a medium by which servants may acquire the benefits proffered by it free from risk, cost, or trouble.

The other objects are : to provide a home for female servants out of place, the usefulness of which hardly requires a word of commendation ; to provide respectable lodgings for men-servants not lodged by their masters ; and to establish a Registry for domestic servants generally, which will form as well a place of advertisement for their services, as a record of their characters, from which they can be obtained upon application.

Any one who is acquainted with the annoyances and inconveniences connected with the present system of " characters to servants," will at once see the importance of the introduction of a system by which the servant will be protected from that ruin which the caprice of a single master (with whom he may even have lived for a short time only) may inflict upon him, and the

master from the risk to which a character wrung
from a former weak master, by the importunities
of an undeserving servant, may expose him.
Nor is it a small benefit to be conferred upon the
servant, to enable him, by appealing to a long
record of former services, to redeem the dis-
qualification which a single fault might bring
upon him.

Should we only succeed in inducing the public
at large to consider all these points, we shall
have the satisfaction of having furthered the
interests of a class which we find recorded in
the Report of the last Census as the most
numerous in the British population.

I shall now call upon the Secretary to lay
before you more in detail the points which I
have slightly touched upon.

AT THE ENTERTAINMENT GIVEN BY

THE MERCHANT TAILORS' COMPANY.

[JUNE 11TH, 1849.]

GENTLEMEN,—

I THANK you sincerely for your expressions
of kindness and cordiality towards me.

Although I have on former occasions met you
in this room, it has always been for some charitable purpose, witnessing with delight the readiness with which this, and indeed all the great
corporations of London, open the doors of their
magnificent Halls at the call of charity. To-day
I am here as a Brother Freeman of your Corporation, fulfilling a promise made from the time
that you received me into your body. I am
ashamed to own how long ago. I beg you not
to measure, by the tardiness of my appearance,
the value which I attach to the honour which
you then conferred upon me, by electing me a
Freeman of the Merchant Tailors' Company.

I remember well with what regret, when,
shortly after I came of age, the Companies of the

Goldsmiths and of the Fishmongers offered me
their freedom, I found myself compelled to
decline this honour, being informed that, iden-
tified as they were by historical tradition, and
still representing two opposite political parties, I
could make a choice only of one of them, and,
fully sensible that, like the Sovereign to whom I
had just been united, and to devote my whole
existence to whom it had become my privilege,
I could belong only to the nation at large, free
from the trammels and above the dissensions of
political parties.

I well remember, too, how much pleased I
was when the two Companies, waiving some of
their statutes, finally agreed both to receive me
amongst them ; and my satisfaction is heightened
when I consider that I owe to that decision the
advantage of finding myself associated with you
also.

Anybody may indeed feel proud to be enrolled
a member of a Company which can boast of
uninterrupted usefulness and beneficence during
four centuries, and holds to this day the same
honourable position in the estimation of the
country which it did in the time of its first formation, although the progress of civilization
and wealth has so vastly raised the community

around it, exemplifying the possibility, in this happy country, of combining the general progress of mankind with a due reverence for the institutions, and even forms, which have been bequeathed to us by the piety and wisdom of our forefathers.

Let us join in the hope that this Corporation may continue in its charitable functions to be equally an object of respect to our children and children's children, and so drink " Prosperity to " the Merchant Tailors' Company."

ON PRESENTING COLOURS TO THE

23RD REGIMENT, ROYAL WELSH FUSILIERS.

[JULY 12TH, 1849.]

––––––––

SOLDIERS OF THE ROYAL WELSH FUSILIERS,

THE ceremony which we are performing this day is a most important, and, to every soldier, a sacred one. It is the transmission to your care and keeping of the Colours which are henceforth to be borne before you, which will be the symbol of your honour, the rallying point in all moments of danger.

I feel most proud to be the person who is to transmit these Colours to a Regiment so renowned for its valour, fortitude, steadiness, and discipline.

In looking over the records of your services, I could not refrain from extracting a few, which show your deeds to have been intimately connected with all the great periods in our history. The Regiment was raised in 1688. Its existence therefore began with the settlement of the liberties of the country. It fought at the Boyne

under Schomberg; captured Namur in Flanders
in 1693; formed part of the great Marlborough's
legions at Blenheim and Oudenarde; fought in
1742 at Dettingen and Fontenoy; decided the
battle of Minden in 1751, for which the name
of *Minden* is inscribed on the colours; showed
examples of valour and perseverance in America
in 1773, at Boston, Charlestown, Brandywine,
and Edgehill; accompanied the Duke of York
to Holland; was amongst the first to land in
Egypt, under the brave Abercrombie, and, later,
the last to embark at Corunna; but between
these two important services fought at Copenhagen, and at the taking of Martinique. *Egypt,
Martinique, and Corunna* are waving in these
Colours. In the Peninsula the Regiment won
for their Colours, under the Duke, the names of
*Albuera, Badajoz, Salamanca, Vittoria, Pyrenees,
Nivelles, Orthes, and Toulouse.* The deeds performed at Albuera are familiar to everybody
who has read Napier's inimitable description of
that action. The Regiment was victorious for
the last time over a powerful enemy at the Duke's
last great victory at Waterloo.

Although you were all of course well acquainted with these glorious records, I have
thought it right to refer to them as a proof that

I

they have not been forgotten by others, and as the best mode of appealing to you to show yourselves at all times worthy of the name you bear.

Take these Colours, one emphatically called the Queen's (let it be a pledge of your loyalty to your Sovereign, and of obedience to the laws of your country); the other, more especially the Regimental one, let that be a pledge of your determination to maintain the honour of your Regiment. In looking at the one, you will think of your Sovereign—in looking at the other, you will think of those who have fought, bled, and conquered before you.

AT THE BANQUET GIVEN BY

THE RIGHT HON. THE LORD MAYOR,

THOMAS FARNCOMBE,

TO HER MAJESTY'S MINISTERS,

FOREIGN AMBASSADORS,

ROYAL COMMISSIONERS OF THE EXHIBITION OF 1851,

AND THE

MAYORS OF ONE HUNDRED AND EIGHTY TOWNS,

AT THE MANSION HOUSE.

[MARCH 21st, 1850.]

MY LORD MAYOR,—

I AM sincerely grateful for the kindness with which you have proposed my health, and to you, gentlemen, for the cordiality with which you have received this proposal.

It must indeed be most gratifying to me to find that a suggestion which I had thrown out, as appearing to me of importance at this time, should have met with such universal concurrence and approbation; for this has proved to me that the view I took of the peculiar character and claims of the time we live in was in accordance with the feelings and opinions of the country.

Gentlemen—I conceive it to be the duty of every educated person closely to watch and study the time in which he lives, and, as far as in him lies, to add his humble mite of individual exertion to further the accomplishment of what he believes Providence to have ordained.

Nobody, however, who has paid any attention to the peculiar features of our present era, will doubt for a moment that we are living at a period of most wonderful transition, which tends rapidly to accomplish that great end, to which, indeed, all history points—*the realization of the unity of mankind*. Not a unity which breaks down the limits and levels the peculiar characteristics of the different nations of the earth, but rather a unity, the *result and product* of those very national varieties and antagonistic qualities.

The distances which separated the different nations and parts of the globe are rapidly vanishing before the achievements of modern invention, and we can traverse them with incredible ease; the languages of all nations are known, and their acquirement placed within the reach of everybody; thought is communicated with the rapidity, and even by the power, of lightning. On the other hand, the *great principle of division of labour*, which may be called the moving power of civilization, is being extended to all branches of science, industry, and art.

Whilst formerly the greatest mental energies strove at universal knowledge, and that knowledge was confined to the few, now they are directed on specialities, and in these, again, even to the minutest points ; but the knowledge acquired becomes at once the property of the community at large ; for, whilst formerly discovery was wrapped in secrecy, the publicity of the present day causes that no sooner is a discovery or invention made than it is already improved upon and surpassed by competing efforts. The products of all quarters of the globe are placed at our disposal, and we have only to choose which is the best and the cheapest for our purposes, and the powers of production are intrusted to the stimulus of *competition and capital.*

So man is approaching a more complete fulfilment of that great and sacred mission which he has to perform in this world. His reason being created after the image of God, he has to use it to discover the laws by which the Almighty governs His creation, and, by making these laws his standard of action, to conquer nature to his use ; himself a divine instrument.

Science discovers these laws of power, motion, and transformation; industry applies them to the raw matter, which the earth yields us in abundance, but which becomes valuable only by knowledge. Art teaches us the immutable laws of beauty and symmetry, and gives to our productions forms in accordance to them.

Gentlemen—the Exhibition of 1851 is to give us a true test and a living picture of the point of development at which the whole of mankind has arrived in this great task, and a new starting-point from which all nations will be able to direct their further exertions.

I confidently hope that the first impression which the view of this vast collection will produce upon the spectator will be that of deep thankfulness to the Almighty for the blessings which He has bestowed upon us already here below ; and the second, the conviction that they can only be realized in proportion to the help which we are prepared to render each other ; therefore, only by peace, love, and ready assistance, not only between individuals, but between the nations of the earth.

This being *my* conviction, I must be highly gratified to see here assembled the magistrates of all the important towns of this realm, sinking all their local and possibly political differences, the representatives of the different political opinions of the country, and the representatives of the different Foreign Nations—to-day representing only *one interest!*

Gentlemen—my original plan had been to carry out this undertaking with the help of the Society of Arts of London, which had long and usefully laboured in this direction, and by the means of private capital and enterprise. You have wished it otherwise, and declared that it was a work which the British people as a whole ought to undertake. I at once yielded to your wishes, feeling that it proceeded from a patriotic, noble, and generous spirit. On *your* courage, perseverance, and liberality, the undertaking now entirely depends. I feel the strongest confidence in these qualities of the British people, and I am sure that they will repose confidence in themselves—confidence that they will honourably sustain the contest of emulation, and that they will nobly carry out their proffered hospitality to their foreign competitors.

We, Her Majesty's Commissioners, are quite

alive to the innumerable difficulties which we shall have to overcome in carrying out the scheme; but, having confidence in you and in our own zeal and perseverance, at least, we require only *your confidence in us* to make us contemplate the result without any apprehension.

AT THE LAYING OF THE FOUNDATION STONE

OF THE

NATIONAL GALLERY AT EDINBURGH.

[AUGUST 30TH, 1850.]

GENTLEMEN,—

NOW that this ceremony is concluded, you must allow me to express to you how much satisfaction it has given me to have had it in my power to comply with your invitation, and to lay the foundation stone of this important National institution, and that this should have coincided with the moment when Her Majesty the Queen has come among you, and has given you a further proof of her attachment to this country, by taking up her abode, if for a short time only, in the ancient palace of her ancestors in this capital, where she has been received with such unequivocal demonstrations of loyalty and affection.

The building, of which we have just begun the foundation, is a temple to be erected to the Fine Arts; the Fine Arts which have so im-

portant an influence upon the development of
the mind and feeling of a people, and which are
so generally taken as the type of the degree and
character of that development, that it is on the
fragments of works of art, come down to us from
bygone nations, that we are wont to form our
estimate of the state of their civilization, manners,
customs, and religion.

Let us hope that the impulse given to the
culture of the Fine Arts in this country, and the
daily increasing attention bestowed upon it by
the people at large, will not only tend to refine
and elevate the national tastes, but will also lead
to the production of works which, if left behind
us as memorials of our age, will give to after
generations an adequate idea of our advanced
state of civilization.

It must be an additional source of gratification
to me to find, that part of the funds rendered
available for the support of this undertaking
should be the ancient grant which, at the union
of the two kingdoms, was secured towards the
encouragement of the fisheries and manufactures
of Scotland, as it affords a most pleasing proof
that those important branches of industry have
arrived at that stage of manhood and prosperity
when, no longer requiring the aid of a fostering

Government, they can maintain themselves independently, relying upon their own vigour and activity, and can now in their turn lend assistance and support to their younger and weaker sisters, the Fine Arts.

Gentlemen, the history of this grant exhibits to us the picture of a most healthy national progress : the ruder arts connected with the necessaries of life *first* gaining strength; then education and science supervening and directing further exertions ; and lastly, the arts which only adorn life becoming longed for by a prosperous and educated people.

May nothing disturb this progress, and may, by God's blessing, that peace and prosperity be preserved to the nation, which will insure to it a long continuance of moral and intellectual enjoyment!

AT THE BANQUET GIVEN BY

THE LORD MAYOR OF YORK,

AND THE MAYORS OF THE CHIEF CITIES AND TOWNS
OF THE UNITED KINGDOM,

TO THE LORD MAYOR OF LONDON.

[OCTOBER 25TH, 1850.]

———

MY LORD MAYOR,—

I AM very sensible of your kindness in proposing my health, and I beg you, gentlemen, to believe that I feel very deeply your demonstrations of good will and cordiality towards myself. I can assure you that I fully reciprocate these sentiments, and that it has given me sincere pleasure to meet you, the representatives of all the important towns of the kingdom, again assembled at a festive board, in token of the unity and harmony of feeling which prevails amongst those whom you represent, and on which, I am persuaded, the happiness and well-being of the country so materially depends.

It was an idea honourable at once to the liberality and the discernment of the Lord

Mayor of London to invite you to assemble under his hospitable roof before you started in the important undertaking upon which you were going to enter; and when, according to ancient custom, the loving-cup went round, it was a pledge you gave each other, that, whatever the rivalries of your different localities might be, you would, in the approaching contest, all act and appear *as one*, representing your country at the gathering of the products of the nations of the earth.

I see by your anxiety to return, before your terms of office shall have expired, the compliment which London has paid you, that you personally appreciate, to its full extent, the intention of its chief magistrate; and you could not have selected a better place for your meeting than this venerable city, which is so much connected with the recollections and the history of the empire, and is now pre-eminent as the centre of a district in which a high state of agriculture is blended with a most extensive production of manufactures.

But I see, likewise, in your anxiety to meet us, Her Majesty's Commissioners, again, a proof of your earnest and continued zeal in the cause of the approaching Exhibition. It could not be by the impetus of a momentary enthusiasm, but only by a steady perseverance and sustained effort, that you could hope to carry out your great undertaking, and ensure for yourselves and the nation an honourable position in the comparison which you have invited.

If, to cheer you on in your labours, by no means terminated, you should require an assurance that that spirit of activity and perseverance *is* abroad in the country, I can give you that assurance on the ground of the information which reaches us from all quarters, and I can add to it our personal conviction, that the works in preparation will be such as to dispel any apprehension for the position which British industry will maintain.

From abroad, also, all the accounts which we receive lead us to expect that the works which are to be sent will be numerous and of a superior character.

Although we perceive, in some countries, a fear that the advantages to be derived from the Exhibition will be mainly reaped by England, and a consequent distrust in the effects of our scheme upon their own interests, we must at the same time freely and gratefully acknowledge that our invitation has been received by all nations, with whom communication was possible, in that spirit of liberality and friendship in which it was tendered, and that they are making great exertions and incurring great expenses in order to meet our plans.

Of our own doings at the Commission I should have preferred to remain silent; but I cannot let this opportunity pass without telling you how much benefit we have derived, in our difficult labours, from your uninterrupted confidence in the intentions, at least, which guided our decisions, and that there has been no difference of opinion on any one subject, between us and the different local Committees, which has not, upon personal consultation, and after open explanation and discussion, vanished, and given way to agreement and identity of purpose.

There is but one alloy to my feelings of satisfaction and pleasure in seeing you here assembled again, and that is, the painful remembrance that one is missing from amongst us who felt so warm an interest in our scheme and took so active a part in promoting its success, the last act of whose public life was attending at the Royal Commission; my admiration for whose talents and character, and gratitude for whose devotion to the Queen, and private friendship towards myself, I feel a consolation in having this public opportunity to express.

Only at our last meeting we were still admiring his eloquence and the earnestness with which he appealed to you to uphold, by your exertions and personal sacrifices, what was to him the highest object—the honour of his country; he met you the following day, together with other Commissioners, to confer with you upon the details of our undertaking; and you must have been struck, as everybody has been who has had the benefit of his advice upon practical points, with the attention, care, and sagacity with which he treated the minutest details, proving that to a great mind nothing is little, from the knowledge that in the moral and intellectual, as in the physical world, the smallest point is only a link in that great chain, and holds its appointed place in that great whole, which is governed by the Divine Wisdom.

The constitution of Sir Robert Peel's mind was peculiarly that of a statesman, and of an English statesman: he was liberal from feeling, but conservative upon principle. Whilst his impulse drove him to foster progress, his sagacious mind and great experience showed him how easily the whole machinery of a state and of society is

deranged, and how important, but how difficult
also, it is to direct its further development in
accordance with its fundamental principles, like
organic growth in nature. It was peculiar to
him, that in great things, as in small, all the
difficulties and objections occurred to him first;
he would anxiously consider them, pause, and
warn against rash resolutions; but having convinced himself, after a long and careful investigation, that a step was not only right to be taken,
but of the practical mode also of safely taking it,
it became to him a necessity and a duty to take
it : all his caution and apparent timidity changed
into courage and power of action, and at the
same time readiness cheerfully to make any
personal sacrifice which its execution might
demand.

Gentlemen, if he has had so great an influence
over this country, it was from the nation recognizing in his qualities the true type of the English
character, which is essentially practical. Warmly
attached to his institutions, and revering the
bequests left to him by the industry, wisdom, and
piety of his forefathers, the Englishman attaches
little value to any theoretical scheme. It will
attract his attention only after having been for

some time placed before him; it must have been thoroughly investigated and discussed before he will entertain it. Should it be an empty theory, it will fall to the ground during this time of probation; should it survive this trial, it will be on account of the practical qualities contained in it; but its adoption in the end will entirely depend upon its harmonizing with the national feeling, the historic development of the country, and the peculiar nature of its institutions.

It is owing to these national qualities that England, whilst constantly progressing, has still preserved the integrity of her constitution from the earliest times, and has been protected from wild schemes whose chief charm lies in their novelty, whilst around us we have seen unfortunately whole nations distracted, and the very fabric of society endangered, from the levity with which the result of the experience of generations, the growth of ages, has been thrown away to give place to temporarily favourite ideas.

Taking this view of the character of our country, I was pleased when I saw the plan of the Exhibition of 1851 undergo its ordeal of doubt, discussion, and even opposition; and I

hope that I may now gather from the energy
and earnestness with which its execution is pursued, that the nation is convinced that it accords
with its interests and the position which England
has taken in the world.

AT THE

DINNER OF THE ROYAL ACADEMY.

[MAY 3RD, 1851.]

MR. PRESIDENT,

MY LORDS AND GENTLEMEN,—

YOU have been very kind in responding with so much warmth to the toast which your President has just proposed to you, and he will allow me to thank him very cordially for the flattering expressions which he used towards myself in introducing to you that toast.

I shall feel very happy if the future should prove that the Great Exhibition, to which all nations have so generously contributed, should, amongst other advantages which I firmly hope will result from it, likewise tend to assist in the promotion of the Fine Arts in this country, of which you are the representatives; and I feel proud that we can show to the many foreigners who are now visiting our shores specimens of British art such as these walls display.

Although I have, since my first arrival in this country, never once missed visiting the Exhibition of the Royal Academy, and have always derived the greatest pleasure and instruction from these visits, it is but seldom that my engagements will allow me to join in your festive dinner. I have, however, upon this occasion, made it a point to do so, in order to assist in what may be considered the inauguration festival of your newly-elected President, at whose election I have heartily rejoiced, not only on account of my high estimate of his qualities, but also on account of my feelings of regard towards him personally.

It would be presumptuous in me to speak to you of his talent as an artist, for that is well known to you, and of it you are the best judges; or of his merits as an author, for you are all familiar with his works, or at least ought to be so; or of his amiable character as a man, for that also you must have had opportunities to estimate: but my connection with him, now for nine years, on Her Majesty's Commission of the Fine Arts, has enabled me to know what you can know less, and what is of the greatest value in a President of the Royal Academy—I mean that kindness of heart and refinement of feeling

which guided him in all his communications,
often most difficult and delicate, with the different
artists whom we had to invite to competition,
whose works we had to criticise, whom we had to
employ or to reject.

Gentlemen, the production of all works in art
or poetry requires, in their conception and execution, not only an exercise of the intellect, skill,
and patience, but particularly *a concurrent warmth
of feeling* and a free flow of imagination. This
renders them most tender plants, which will
thrive only in an atmosphere calculated to maintain that warmth, and that atmosphere is one of
kindness—kindness towards the artist personally
as well as towards his production. An unkind
word of criticism passes like a cold blast over
their tender shoots, and shrivels them up, checking the flow of the sap, which was rising to
produce, perhaps, multitudes of flowers and fruit.
But still criticism is absolutely necessary to the
development of art, and the injudicious praise of
an inferior work becomes an insult to superior
genius.

In this respect our times are peculiarly unfavourable when compared with those when
Madonnas were painted in the seclusion of convents; for we have now on the one hand the

eager competition of a vast array of artists of
every degree of talent and skill, and on the other,
as judge, a great public, for the greater part
wholly uneducated in art, and thus led by professional writers, who often strive to impress the
public with a great idea of their own artistic
knowledge by the merciless manner in which
they treat works which cost those who produced
them the highest efforts of mind or feeling.

The works of art, by being publicly exhibited
and offered for sale, are becoming articles of
trade, following as such the unreasoning laws of
markets and fashion; and public and even private patronage is swayed by their tyrannical
influence.

It is, then, to an institution like this, gentlemen, that we must look for a counterpoise to
these evils. Here young artists are educated
and taught the mysteries of their profession;
those who have distinguished themselves, and
given proof of their talent and power, receive
a badge of acknowledgment from their professional brethren by being elected Associates of
the Academy; and are at last, after long toil and
continued exertion, received into a select aristocracy of a limited number, and shielded in any
further struggle by their well-established reputa-

tion, of which the letters R.A. attached to their
names give a pledge to the public.

If this body is often assailed from without, it
shares only the fate of every aristocracy; if more
than another, this only proves that it is even
more difficult to sustain an aristocracy of merit
than one of birth or of wealth, and may serve as
a useful check upon yourselves when tempted at
your elections to let personal predilection compete with real merit.

Of one thing, however, you may rest assured,
and that is the continued favour of the Crown.
The same feelings which actuated George the
Third in founding this institution, still actuate
the Crown in continuing to it its patronage and
support, recognizing in you a constitutional link,
as it were, between the Crown itself and the
artistic body. And when I look at the assem-
blage of guests at this table, I may infer that the
Crown does not stand alone in this respect, but
that its feelings are shared also by the great and
noble in the land.

May the Academy long flourish, and continue
its career of usefulness!

AT THE THIRD JUBILEE OF

THE INCORPORATED SOCIETY

FOR THE

PROPAGATION OF THE GOSPEL IN FOREIGN PARTS.

[JUNE 16TH, 1851.]

My Lords, Ladies, and Gentlemen,—

WE are assembled here to-day in order to celebrate the third jubilee of the foundation of the " Society for the Propagation of the " Gospel in Foreign Parts," incorporated by Royal Charter, and one of the chief sources of the spiritual aid which the Church of England affords to our extensive colonial dependencies.

We are not commemorating, however, an isolated fact which may have been glorious or useful to the country, but we are thankfully acknowledging the Divine favour which has attended exertions which have been unremitting during the lapse of one hundred and fifty years. We are met at the same time to invoke the further continuance of that favour, pledging ourselves

not to relax in our efforts to extend to those of
our brethren who are settled in distant lands,
and building up communities and states where
man's footsteps had first to be imprinted on the
soil, and wild nature yet to be conquered to his
use, those blessings of Christianity which form
the foundation of our community and of our
state.

This Society was first chartered by that great
man William the Third, the greatest sovereign this
country has to boast of; by whose sagacity and
energy was closed that bloody struggle for civil
and religious liberty which so long had con-
vulsed this country, and who secured to us the
inestimable advantages of our constitution and
of our Protestant faith.

Having thus placed the country upon a safe
basis at home, he could boldly meet her foes
abroad, and contribute to the foundation of that
colonial empire which forms so important a part
of our present greatness; and honour be to him
for his endeavour to place this foundation upon
the rock of the Church.

The first jubilee of the Society fell in times
when religious apathy had succeeded to the over-
excitement of the preceding age. Lax morals
and a sceptical philosophy began to undermine

the Christian faith, treating with indifference and even ridicule the most sacred objects. Still this Society persevered in its labours with unremitting zeal, turning its chief attention to the North American continent, where a young and vigorous society was rapidly growing into a people.

The second jubilee found this country in a most critical position : she had obtained, by the peace of Amiens, a moment's respite from the tremendous contest in which she had been engaged with her continental rival, and which she had soon to renew, in order to maintain her own existence, and to secure a permanent peace to Europe. Since the last jubilee, the American colonies, which had originally been peopled chiefly by British subjects who had left their homes to escape the yoke of religious intolerance and oppression, had thrown off their allegiance to the mother country in defence of civil rights, the attachment to which they had carried with them from the British soil. Yet this Society was not dismayed, but in a truly Christian spirit continued its labours in the neighbouring North American and West Indian settlements.

This, the third jubilee, falls in a happier epoch, when peace is established in Europe, and religious fervour is rekindled, and at an auspicious moment when we are celebrating a festival of the civilization of mankind, to which all quarters of the globe have contributed their productions, and are sending their people, for the first time recognizing their advancement as a common good, their interests as identical, their mission on earth the same.

And this civilization rests on Christianity, could only be raised on Christianity, can only be maintained by Christianity! the blessings of which are now carried by this Society to the vast territories of India and Australasia, which last are again to be peopled by the Anglo-Saxon race.

Whilst we have thus to congratulate ourselves upon our state of temporal prosperity, harmony at home, and peace abroad, we cannot help deploring that the Church, whose exertions for the progress of Christianity and civilization we are to-day acknowledging, should be afflicted by internal dissensions and attacks from without. I have no fear, however, for her safety and ultimate welfare so long as she holds fast to what our ancestors gained for us at the Reformation— *the Gospel and the unfettered right of its use.*

The dissensions and difficulties which we wit-

ness in this as in every other Church arise from
the natural and necessary conflict of the two
antagonistic principles which move human society in Church as well as in State; I mean the
principles of *individual liberty and of allegiance
and submission to the will of the community*, ex-
acted by it for its own preservation.

These conflicting principles cannot safely be
disregarded: they must be reconciled. To this
country belongs the honour of having succeeded
in this mighty task, as far as the State is concerned, whilst other nations are still wrestling
with it; and I feel persuaded that the same earnest zeal and practical wisdom which has made
her political Constitution an object of admiration
to other nations will, under God's blessing, make
her Church likewise a model to the world.

Let us look upon this assembly as a token of
future hope; and may the harmony which reigns
amongst us at this moment, and which we owe
to having met in furtherance of a common holy
object, be by the Almighty permanently bestowed
upon the Church.

AT THE

ROYAL AGRICULTURAL SOCIETY'S SHOW.

[WINDSOR, JULY 16TH, 1851.]

My Lord Duke,
My Lords and Gentlemen,—

I AM very sensible of the honour which you have done me in proposing my health; and I can assure you, gentlemen, that the kind way in which you have responded to the toast will never be forgotten by me.

Some years have elapsed already since I last dined with you in this migratory pavilion, and I am glad that you should have pitched it this day under the walls of Windsor Castle, and that I should myself have an opportunity of bidding you a hearty welcome in the Home Park.

Your encampment singularly contrasts with that which the barons of England, the feudal lords of the land, with their retainers, erected round old Windsor Castle on a similar mead, though not exactly in the same locality. They came then clad in steel, with lance and war-horse;

you appear in a more peaceful attire, and the
animals you bring with you are the tokens of
your successful cultivation of the arts of peace.
King John came trembling amongst his subjects,
unwillingly compelled to sign that Great Charter
which has ever since been your birthright. Your
Sovereign came confiding among her loyal and
loving people; she came to admire the results of
their industry, and to encourage them to perse-
vere in their exertions.

And the gratification which the Queen has felt
at the sight of your splendid collection must, I
am sure, be participated in by all who examine
it. I am doubly pleased at this success, not only
because it is witnessed by the many visitors from
foreign lands now within our shores, whom every
Englishman must wish to inspire with respect
for the state of British agriculture, but also because I feel to a certain degree personally responsible for having deprived you of one generally most interesting feature of your show:
I mean the field-fruits and the agricultural
machines and implements. Though separated
from your collection, they are seen to great advantage in another Royal Park; and you will
have been glad to hear that, " whatever the diffi-
" culty may be in deciding upon the superiority

" of the works of industry and art sent to the
" Crystal Palace by the different nations of the
" earth, the British agricultural implements are
" acknowledged by common consent to stand
" there almost without a rival."

Let me now use the privilege which your President has allowed me to enjoy, in proposing to you, as a toast, " Prosperity to the Royal Agri-
" cultural Society."   To its exhibitions, the means of comparison which they have afforded, and the emulation which they have stimulated, we owe to a great extent the progress which British agriculture has made of late.   To this Society belongs the honour to have been one of the first to appreciate the value of such exhibitions, and to have from the beginning liberally and fearlessly admitted all competitors without restriction.

I drink, " Prosperity to the Royal Agricul-
" tural Society."

BANQUET AT THE TRINITY HOUSE.

[JUNE 4TH, 1853.]

1.

WHEREVER Englishmen meet at a public dinner they make it their pride to take no proceedings without first drinking to the health of " The Queen." The Corporation of the Trinity House yield in feelings of loyalty to none of Her Majesty's subjects.—Gentlemen !

"THE QUEEN ! "

2.

The toast I have now to propose to you is that of the Royal Family.

It is a blessing attending the monarchical institutions of this country, that the domestic relations and the domestic happiness of the sovereign are inseparable from the relations and happiness of the people at large. In the progress

L

of the Royal Family through life is reflected, as it were, the progress of the generation to which they belong, and out of the common sympathy felt for them arises an additional bond of union amongst the people themselves. I have often been deeply touched by the many proofs of kindness, and, I may say, almost parental affection, with which the Prince of Wales and the rest of our young family have been welcomed on their earliest appearance. May God grant that they may some day repay that affection, and make themselves worthy of it by fulfilling the expectations which the country so fondly cherishes!

3.

I am sure that you could not have entered this room without feeling a pang at missing from the chair, which I am this day called upon to occupy, that great man whose loss we still find it almost impossible to realise. It would be repugnant to our feelings to take another step in the proceedings of this evening without paying a mournful tribute to his name. Let us drink in solemn silence to the memory of the great Duke, to whom this Corporation, as well as the whole nation, are so deeply indebted.

4.

I have now to invite you to drink to the British Army and Navy, and in doing so I would add to the toast the names of the two distinguished men who preside over them, the General Commanding-in-Chief and the First Lord of the Admiralty, Viscount Hardinge and Sir James Graham.

It is under the protection of these two great services that this country has attained an extent of power, wealth, and territory, without a parallel in history.

We are rich, prosperous, and contented, therefore peaceful by instinct.

We are becoming, I hope, daily more civilized and religious, and, therefore, daily recognizing more and more, that the highest use to which we can apply the advantages with which an all-bountiful Providence has favoured us, is to extend and maintain the blessings of Peace. I hope, however, the day may never arrive which would find us either so enervated by the enjoyment of riches and luxury, or so sunk in the decrepitude of age, that, from a miserable eagerness to cling to our mere wealth and comforts, we should be deaf to the calls of Honour and Duty.

5.

The Health of Her Majesty's Ministers is the toast which I now ask you to drink.

The Brethren of the Trinity House have at all times been anxious cordially to co-operate with Her Majesty's Government, by whomsoever conducted ; they know no politics, but feel that the responsibility which is imposed upon those men who are intrusted with the care of the multifarious interests of this vast empire is an awful one, requiring every assistance which it may be in the power of individuals or public bodies to afford. They are convinced also, that, however party violence may separate public men from each other, they are all equally influenced by one sole consideration, the good of their country.

The Earl of Aberdeen and Her Majesty's Ministers.

6.

I am very grateful to you, gentlemen, for the kindness with which you have received the toast proposed by the Deputy Master, and beg to thank him for the obliging terms in which he has proposed my health.

When this important Corporation elected me as their Master, I was well aware that I did not owe this to any personal merit of my own, giving me a claim to such an honour, and I might well have paused before I undertook to succeed, in any task or position, that great Man whom few can hope to equal in talent, energy, and wisdom; but I saw in the choice of the Brethren a desire to mark their attachment to the Throne, and, in my own acceptance, a means for the Queen to testify through me her interest and solicitude for British Commerce and Shipping, and for the British Seaman. This Corporation has had, since King Henry the Eighth, one of the high functions of administration delegated to it by the State, that, namely, of lighting the coast, piloting vessels, and tendering aid and assistance to the merchant seaman worn out by the toils and the privations of his adventurous life. The world bears testimony to the manner in which this duty has been discharged; and I can refer to none which can be more satisfactory to the Corporation than that which has been only recently borne by our brethren on the other side of the Atlantic.

Gentlemen! The ever-changing, renovating, and preserving influences of time have, in their

inevitable operation, made themselves felt also
with regard to this Institution, and the greatest
credit is due to the wisdom and patriotism of the
Brethren for having rightly judged and appreciated the demands made by them. Having
hitherto enjoyed the almost irresponsible power
of taxing the public for the objects of their trust,
they cheerfully consented to submit their affairs
to the utmost publicity, as well as to a control
from Government. Their own power they
surrendered without a murmur; the interests of
the poor seaman they thought themselves bound
to advocate. Whilst repudiating any wish to
retain patronage in the distribution of alms,
which in fact they had hitherto looked upon
rather as an anxious and responsible duty, they
exerted themselves to the utmost to bring the
claims of this deserving class before the Government; and whatever may be the inherent
difficulty in framing a measure, the purport of
which is to relieve a *class*, without impairing its
moral strength and self-dependence, they still
hope that the Legislature will not shrink from
the attempt.

Gentlemen—for all the Trinity House may
have done, thanks are solely due to the excellent
Deputy Master, and the Elder Brethren by whom

he is so efficiently supported. Let us drink his health, and Prosperity to the Corporation of the Trinity House.

7.

One of the peculiar features of the public life of this country is, that no public body stands isolated in the community, but that it endeavours to establish and maintain an organic connection with the other interests and classes of society, securing thereby the inestimable advantage of harmony of action and feeling. The Corporation of the Trinity House has sought to effect this through its Honorary Brethren; and I have only to point to those who now sit as such round this table to prove that, whilst the Corporation has been guided in its choice solely by the desire to connect itself with the men who stand highest in the estimation of their country, the most distinguished men have, on their side, deemed it an honour to become the objects of that choice.

In drinking to the Honorary Brethren, I would mention the name of the gallant Admiral of the Fleet, Sir Byam Martin, who may be truly called the Father of his profession.

AT THE BICENTENARY FESTIVAL OF THE

CORPORATION OF THE SONS OF THE CLERGY.

[MAY 10TH, 1854.]

My Lord Mayor,—

ALLOW me to return you, on my own behalf, and on that of the Royal Family, my best thanks for the manner in which you have proposed our health, and to you, gentlemen, for the cordial response which you have made to the toast.

I am, indeed, highly gratified to have been a witness to the *Two Hundredth Anniversary* of this Festival, testifying, as it does, that the people of this country do not relax in efforts which they have once undertaken, and do not forsake the spirit which animated their forefathers.

When our ancestors purified the Christian faith, and shook off the yoke of a domineering Priesthood, they felt that the key-stone of that wonderful fabric which had grown up in the dark times of the middle ages was the *Celibacy of the Clergy*, and shrewdly foresaw that their reformed faith and newly-won religious liberty would, on the contrary, only be secure in the hands of a clergy united with the people by every sympathy, national, personal, and domestic.

Gentlemen—this nation has enjoyed for three hundred years the blessing of a Church Establishment which rests upon this basis, and cannot be too grateful for the advantages afforded by the fact that the Christian Ministers not only preach the *doctrines* of Christianity, but live among their congregations an example for the discharge of every *Christian duty*, as husbands, fathers, and masters of families, themselves capable of fathoming the whole depth of human feelings, desires, and difficulties.

Whilst we must gratefully acknowledge that they have, as a body, worthily fulfilled this high and difficult task, we must bear in mind that we deny them an equal participation in one of the actuating motives of life—the one which, amongst the " children of this generation," exercises, perhaps of necessity, the strongest influence—I mean the desire for the acquisition and accumulation of the goods of this world.

Gentlemen—the appellation of a " money-

" making parson " is not only a reproach but a
condemnation for a clergyman, depriving him at
once of all influence over his congregation. Yet
this man, who has to shun opportunities for
acquiring wealth open to most of us, and who
has himself only an often scanty life-income
allotted to him for his services, has a wife and
children like ourselves ; and we wish him to
have the same solicitude for their welfare which
we feel for our own.

Are we not bound, then, to do what we can to
relieve his mind from anxiety, and to preserve
his children from destitution, when it shall have
pleased the Almighty to remove him from the
scene of his labours ?

You have given an answer in the affirmative
by your presence here to-day ; and although this
institution can do *materially* but little, morally it
gives a public recognition of the claims which
the sons of the clergy have upon the sympathy
and liberality of the community at large, and as
such is of the greatest value.

May it continue for further hundreds of years
as a band of union between Clergy and Laity,
and on each recurring centenary may it find this
nation ever advancing in prosperity, civilization,
and piety !

DINNER AT THE TRINITY HOUSE.

[JUNE 21st, 1854.]

1.
" THE QUEEN."

2.

THE toast which I have to propose to you is that of—

" His Royal Highness the PRINCE OF WALES
" and the rest of the ROYAL FAMILY."

In doing so, I am impelled to refer to one Member of that family who is at present engaged in the discharge of arduous duties in the East. He is the only one whom both his position and his age permitted to offer his services on this occasion, and I rejoice at his having done so, as a proof that the Members of the Royal Family are at all times ready to serve—ay! and, if necessary, to bleed for their country.

3.

" The Army and Navy."

The toast which I have now to propose to you —" The Army and Navy of Great Britain "— will be drunk by you with peculiar emotions at this time, as your eyes are turned towards these Services, your hearts beat for them, and with their success the welfare and the honour of the country are so intimately bound up.

They will do their duty as they have always done, and may the Almighty bless their efforts!

What is asked to be achieved by them in this instance is a task of inordinate difficulty, not only from the nature and climate of the country in which they are fighting, but also from the peculiarity of the enemy to whom they are opposed, as it may so happen that the Army may meet a foe of ten times its number, whilst the Fleet may find it impossible to meet one at all.

All these difficulties, however, may be considered as compensated by the goodness of our cause, " the vindication of the public law of " Europe," and the fact that we have fighting by our side a Power, the military prowess and vigour of which we have hitherto chiefly known from the severity of long and anxious contests.

If there be a contest between us now, it will be one of emulation, and not of enmity.

" The Army and Navy of Great Britain, and " the Health of the Right Honourable Lord " VISCOUNT HARDINGE, and the Right Honour- " able SIR JAMES GRAHAM, Bart."

4.

We are honoured to-day by the presence of the Members of Her Majesty's Government. The only return which the country can make to those men, who sacrifice their own quiet, privacy, and often health, to the arduous and anxious labours of conducting the public business, is an acknowledgment of the sincerity and disinterestedness of their motives of action. This it is which I invite you to give upon the present occasion in drinking the health of Her Majesty's Government, and LORD JOHN RUSSELL, Lord President of the Council.

6.

I am very much obliged to you for the kind expressions in which you have proposed my health, and to the company for the way in which they have received it. But I have to thank you, the Elder Brethren, especially, for the mark of confidence which you have shown me in re-electing me as your Master, a confidence which I assure you that I appreciate highly, and of which I shall be anxious to prove myself at all times worthy. Although the duties of my office are hardly more than nominal, I attach the greatest value to my personal connection with your Corporation — the only public body to whom duties are intrusted so deeply affecting the interests of the commerce, the shipping, and the seamen of this country. I must also take this opportunity to congratulate you on the working of the important alterations made last year in your constitution, as they have proved a successful attempt at that difficult and nice operation, to bring the spontaneous activity of a public body into harmony with the general feelings of the country, as represented in its Government, without destroying all individual and organic life by the killing influence of an arbitrary mechanical centralization.

In proposing to you to drink to the future prosperity of the Corporation, I shall but follow your wishes in coupling the toast with the name

of the Deputy-Master, to whose zeal and ability
so much of its present prosperity is due.

7.

I have the honour of naming to you, as the
next toast, " The Honorary Brethren of the
" Corporation." They are composed of men,
although varying in their political opinions, yet
all standing high in the estimation of their
country—an esteem which they have earned by
distinguished services rendered to the State, and
the Corporation is justly proud of its connection
with them. I would ask permission to couple
the toast with the name of The Earl of Had-
dington.

14.

In returning the thanks of the Corporation to
our distinguished guests, I beg leave to propose
to you " The Health of the Lord High Chan-
" cellor of England, and the other noble and
" distinguished persons who have this day
" honoured the Corporation by their presence."

SPEECHES DELIVERED AT THE

ANNUAL DINNER AT THE TRINITY-HOUSE.

[JUNE 9TH, 1855.]

———

1.

"THE QUEEN!"

2.

I PROPOSE to you the health of the PRINCE of WALES and the rest of the ROYAL FAMILY. May they prosper under the favour of the Almighty!

3.

The toast which I now propose to you—the "Army and Navy"—is one in which I am sure no Englishman can join at this moment without the feelings of the deepest emotion. In their keeping stand the honour and the best interests of this country—I may say the interests of the civilization of Europe. And nobly have they done their duty! whether in the daring impetuosity of

attack, in the cool intrepidity of defence, or the
noble and truly Christian patience with which they
have endured nameless sufferings and privations !
They have set us all an example well worthy of
imitation, and making us proud of the generation to which we belong.   May God grant that
their exertions may be crowned with the success
they have striven to deserve, and that they may,
by the side of our noble and gallant allies, conquer to the world a peace which may secure its
tranquillity and prosperity from any further
interruption !

I drink " The health of Viscount Hardinge,
" Sir Charles Wood, and the Army and Navy.
" Success to their exertions !"

4.

I now propose to you the health of " Her Ma-
" jesty's Ministers."

If there ever was a time when the Queen's
Government, by whomsoever conducted, required
the support—ay, not the support alone, but the
confidence, goodwill, and sympathy of their fellow
countrymen, it is the present.   It is not the way
to success in war to support it, however ardently
and energetically, and to run down and weaken
those who have to conduct it.   We are engaged

M

with a mighty adversary, who uses against us
all those wonderful powers which have sprung
up under the generating influence of our liberty
and our civilization, and employs them with all
the force which unity of purpose and action,
impenetrable secresy, and uncontrolled despotic
power give him ; whilst we have to meet him
under a state of things intended for peace and the
promotion of that very civilization—a civilization
the offspring of public discussion, the friction of
parties, and popular control over the government
of the State.   The Queen has no power to levy
troops, and none at her command, except such
as voluntarily offer their services.   Her Government can entertain no measures for the prosecution of the war without having to explain them
publicly in Parliament; her armies and fleets
can make no movement, nor even prepare for
any, without its being proclaimed by the press ;
and no mistake, however trifling, can occur, no
weakness exist, which it may be of the utmost
importance to conceal from the world, without
its being publicly denounced, and even frequently exaggerated, with a morbid satisfaction.
The Queen's ambassadors can carry on no nego-
ciation which has not to be publicly defended by
entering into all the arguments which a nego-

ciator, to have success, must be able to shut up
in the innermost recesses of his heart—nay, at
the most critical moment, when the complication
of military measures and diplomatic negociations
may be at their height, an adverse vote in Parliament may of a sudden deprive her of all her
confidential servants.

Gentlemen ! Constitutional Government is
under a heavy trial, and can only pass triumph-
antly through it, if the country will grant its
confidence—a patriotic, indulgent, and self-denying confidence—to Her Majesty's Government.
Without this, all their labours must be in vain.

I hope you will drink with me " The Health
" of Viscount Palmerston and Her Majesty's
" Ministers."

5.

I am much obliged to you for your kindness
in proposing my health, and to the company for
the reception which they have given to the
toast.

It always affords me great satisfaction to be
able to preside at your annual Dinner, particularly when I can congratulate you on the com-
pletion of another year of usefulness and of successful labour. This I am enabled to do on the

present occasion, and have only to point to the
satisfactory working of your extended jurisdiction
over the Cinque Port pilots—to the progress of
your lighthouses—to the success in your efforts to
ameliorate the condition of the ballast-heavers—
and to the fact that you have, through the
Board of Trade, entered into a communication
with Her Majesty's Colonies, for the purpose of
laying down a complete system of lighting, based
on your knowledge and experience, in those
important but remotely-removed parts of the
world.

It is to the indefatigable zeal of the Deputy-
Master that much of this success is due; you
will, therefore, I doubt not, gladly join with me
in drinking to *his good health*, in connection
with the toast of the evening—" Prosperity to
" the Corporation of the Trinity House."

AT THE OPENING OF

THE NEW CATTLE MARKET,

IN COPENHAGEN FIELDS, ISLINGTON.

[JUNE 13TH, 1855.]

My Lord Mayor and Gentlemen,—

ACCEPT the expression of my hearty thanks for your kind welcome, and for the gratifying assurance of your loyal and affectionate attachment to the Queen and her Family. I have been much pleased by the opportunity which your kind invitation has afforded me of seeing and admiring the great work which you this day open to the public—a work which not only deserves all admiration in itself, on account of the excellence of the arrangements and the magnificence of the design, but which will, I trust, be found eminently conducive to the comfort and health of the City of London. That its success will be commensurate with the spirit in which it has been undertaken and carried out I cannot doubt. A certain dislocation of habits

and interests must inevitably attend the removal
of the great City market from the site it has
occupied for so many centuries, and this may
possibly retard for the moment the fullest development of the undertaking; but any opposition
arising from such causes will soon cease, and the
farmers will, doubtless, soon learn to appreciate
the boon thus conferred upon them by the Corporation of London in the increased facility
which will be afforded to them for the transaction
of their business and the comparative security
with which they will be enabled to bring up and
display their valuable stock in the Great Metropolitan Cattle Market.

[The LORD MAYOR gave the health of HIS ROYAL HIGHNESS,
who, in responding to the toast, said]—

MY LORD MAYOR,—

I RETURN you my best thanks for the honour
you have done me in proposing my health,
and to you, gentlemen, for the kindness with
which you have responded to the toast.

It has given me very great pleasure to have
been able to accept the invitation of the Lord
Mayor to be present at the opening of this
splendid and useful work; and I beg to assure

him that the oftener he shall invite me to similar
ceremonies, the better I shall be pleased.

This wonderful metropolis, which has already
gathered beneath its roofs nearly two million
and a half of human beings, and has even within
these last six years added not less than 290 miles
of street to its extent, imperatively requires that
those establishments which are to minister to the
common wants of the whole should keep pace
with its growth and magnitude. They can only
be undertaken by public bodies, they can only
be successfully carried out by public spirit. I
know that the difficulties which have to be overcome, where so much private capital has acquired
vested interests, are immense ; but I hail the
spirit which is rising amongst us, and which, I
doubt not, will meet those difficulties. I hail this
instance as an earnest of your determination to
accept the duties which your position has imposed
upon you, and as a proof that success will at all
times reward a bold and conscientious execution
of them.

I beg now to propose to you to drink the
" Health of the Lord Mayor and Corporation of
" the City of London, and Prosperity to the New
" Metropolitan Cattle Market."

AT THE BANQUET IN

THE BIRMINGHAM TOWN HALL,

ON THE OCCASION OF LAYING THE FIRST STONE

OF THE

BIRMINGHAM AND MIDLAND INSTITUTE.

[NOVEMBER 22ND, 1855.]

[An Address having been presented by the Corporation,

His ROYAL HIGHNESS in reply said—]

MR. MAYOR AND GENTLEMEN,—

THE cordial reception I have met with from you demands my warmest acknowledgments. You only, I assure you, do me justice in giving me credit for a deep interest in whatever may tend to promote the advancement of either the moral or the material good of the people of this country; but you are doing so in too flattering a manner, and attach too high a value to any service that it may have been in my power to render in this cause. I feel it would be a high privilege to be associated in any way with those who are making such noble

efforts — and nowhere with more energy and
perseverance than in Birmingham — for the
improvement of their fellow-countrymen ; and
to be allowed to witness the success of those
efforts will be a more than sufficient reward for
any assistance I may myself have been enabled
to afford.

[Lord CALTHORPE having read the Address of the Council of
the Institute,

His ROYAL HIGHNESS said—]

MY LORDS AND GENTLEMEN,—

I THANK you very sincerely for your address.
It is with more than ordinary pleasure that I
have accepted your kind invitation to take part
in the ceremony which is this day to mark the
first step towards the establishment of an Institution, from which I join with its warmest supporters
in looking for the most advantageous results.

I cannot, indeed, doubt for a moment that the
expectations of those who believe that the " value
" and dignity of human labour will receive a
" manifold increase, when guided by the light
" of scientific knowledge," will be amply realized.
And it is most gratifying to me to hear the
expression of your opinion that the desire for the
" keener and more comprehensive study of the
" principles by which the exercise of man's pro-

" ductive powers is controlled," from which you
anticipate such advantage, has been stimulated by
the Great Exhibition of 1851, to my connection
with which you have been pleased to allude in
such flattering terms.

I cannot forget that the example of such Industrial Exhibitions had been already set by this
town, and with the best results ; or that to the
experience so acquired the Executive Committee
of the greater undertaking of '51 were much
indebted in carrying that work to a successful
issue. As Birmingham was thus foremost in
giving a practical stimulus to the works of Art
and Industry, so she is now one of the first in
the field to encourage a scientific study of the
principles on which those works depend for
success.

I trust with you, and confidently believe, that
the moral as well as the material welfare of this
great community will be advanced by the union,
for scientific objects, of men of all classes and of
all opinions, in such institutions as that of which
I am to-day to have the honour of laying the
first stone. And most heartily do I join with
you in congratulating the country that not even
such a war as that in which we are now engaged,
calculated as it is to enlist our warmest sympathies

and to engage our more immediate interest, can divert Englishmen from the noble work of fostering the Arts of Peace, and endeavouring to give a wider scope to the blessings of freedom and civilization.

[Lord CALTHORPE, the President of the Institute, proposed " The Health of PRINCE ALBERT, and the other Members " of the Royal Family."

HIS ROYAL HIGHNESS replied—]

I AM much obliged to you, my Lord, for your proposing my health in such kind terms, and I cannot but be much gratified by the cordial reception which you, gentlemen, have been pleased to give to this toast.

It has been a great pleasure to me to have been able to participate, in however trifling a degree, in a work which I do not look upon as a simple act of worldly wisdom on the part of this great town and locality, but as one of the first public acknowledgments of a principle which is daily forcing its way amongst us, and is destined to play a great and important part in the future development of this nation and of the world in general : I mean the introduction of science and art as the unconscious regulators of productive industry.

The courage and spirit of enterprise with

which an immense amount of capital is embarked
in industrial pursuits, and the skill and indefatigable perseverance with which these are carried
on in this country, cannot but excite universal
admiration; but in all our operations, whether
agricultural or manufacturing, it is not *we* who
operate, but the laws of nature, which we have
set in operation.

It is, then, of the highest importance that we
should know these laws, in order to know what
we are about, and the reason why certain things
are, which occur daily under our hands, and what
course we are to pursue with regard to them.

Without such knowledge we are condemned
to one of three states: either we merely go on to
do things just as our fathers did, and for no
better reason than because they did them so; or,
trusting to some personal authority, we adopt at
random the recommendation of some specific, in
a speculative hope that it may answer; or lastly
—and this is the most favourable case—we ourselves improve upon certain processes; but this
can only be the result of an experience hardly
earned and dearly bought, and which, after all,
can only embrace a comparatively short space of
time, and a small number of experiments.

From none of these causes can we hope for

much progress; for the mind, however ingenious, has no materials to work with, and remains
in presence of phenomena, the causes of which
are hidden from it.

But these laws of nature, these divine laws, are
capable of being discovered and understood, and
of being taught and made our own. *This is the
task of science*; and, whilst science discovers and
teaches these laws, art teaches their application.
No pursuit is therefore too insignificant not to
be capable of becoming the subject both of a
science and an art.

The fine arts (as far as they relate to painting, sculpture, and architecture), which are sometimes confounded with art in general, rest on the
application of the laws of form and colour, and
what may be called the science of the beautiful.
They do not rest on any arbitrary theory on the
modes of producing pleasurable emotions, but
follow fixed laws—more difficult perhaps to seize
than those regulating the material world, because
belonging partly to the sphere of the ideal, and
of our spiritual essence, yet perfectly appreciable
and teachable, both abstractedly and historically,
from the works of different ages and nations.

No human pursuits make any material progress until science is brought to bear upon them.

We have seen accordingly many of them slumber for centuries upon centuries ; but from the moment that science has touched them with her magic wand, they have sprung forward, and taken strides which amaze, and almost awe, the beholder.

Look at the transformation which has gone on around us since the laws of gravitation, electricity, magnetism, and the expansive power of heat have become known to us. It has altered our whole state of existence,—one might say, the whole face of the globe. We owe this to science, and to science alone ; and she has other treasures in store for us, if we will but call her to our assistance.

It is sometimes objected by the ignorant that science is uncertain and changeable, and they point with a malicious kind of pleasure to the many exploded theories which have been superseded by others, as a proof that the present knowledge may be also unsound, and, after all, not worth having. But they are not aware that, while they think to cast blame upon science, they bestow, in fact, the highest praise upon her.

For that is precisely the difference between science and prejudice : that the latter keeps stubbornly to its position, whether disproved or not, whilst the former is an unarrestable movement towards the fountain of truth, caring little for cherished authorities or sentiments, but continually progressing, feeling no false shame at her shortcomings, but, on the contrary, the highest pleasure, when freed from an error, at having advanced another step towards the attainment of Divine truth—a pleasure not even intelligible to the pride of ignorance.

We also hear, not unfrequently, science and practice, scientific knowledge and common sense, contrasted as antagonistic. A strange error! for science is eminently practical, and must be so, as she sees and knows what she is doing, whilst mere common practice is condemned to work in the dark, applying natural ingenuity to unknown powers to obtain a known result.

Far be it from me to undervalue the creative power of genius, or to treat shrewd common sense as worthless without knowledge. But nobody will tell me that the same genius would not take an incomparably higher flight, if supplied with all the means which knowledge can impart; or that common sense does not become, in fact, only truly powerful when in possession of the materials upon which judgment is to be exercised.

The study of the laws by which the Almighty governs the Universe is therefore our bounden duty. Of these laws our great academies and seats of education have, rather arbitrarily, selected only two spheres or groups (as I may call them) as essential parts of our national education : the laws which regulate quantities and proportions, which form the subject of mathematics, and the laws regulating the expression of our thoughts, through the medium of language, that is to say, grammar, which finds its purest expression in the classical languages. These laws are most important branches of knowledge, their study trains and elevates the mind, but they are not the only ones; there are others which we cannot disregard, which we cannot do without.

There are, for instance, the laws governing the human mind, and its relation to the Divine Spirit (the subject of logic and metaphysics) ; there are those which govern our bodily nature and its connection with the soul (the subject of physiology and psychology) ; those which govern human society, and the relations between man and man (the subjects of politics, jurisprudence, and political economy); and many others.

Whilst of the laws just mentioned some have been recognized as essentials of education in different institutions, and some will, by the course of time, more fully assert their right to recognition, the laws regulating matter and form are those which will constitute the chief object of *your* pursuits; and, as the principal of subdivision of labour is the one most congenial to our age, I would advise you to keep to this speciality, and to follow with undivided attention chiefly the sciences of mechanics, physics, and chemistry, and the fine arts in painting, sculpture, and architecture.

You will thus have conferred an inestimable boon upon your country, and in a short time have the satisfaction of witnessing the beneficial results upon our national powers of production. Other parts of the country will, I doubt not, emulate your example; and I live in hope that all these institutions will some day find a central point of union, and thus complete their national organization.

Thanking you once more for having allowed me to assist at the foundation of your Institution, I, with all my heart, wish it growth, vigour, and prosperity.

N

ADDRESS TO THE

3RD AND 4TH REGIMENTS OF THE GERMAN LEGION

AT SHORNCLIFFE, ON PRESENTING TO THEM
THEIR COLOURS.

[DECEMBER 6TH, 1855.]

———

ES freut mich herzlich Ihnen persönlich diese Fahnen überreichen zu können, da mir diess zugleich eine Gelegenheit giebt Ihnen auszudrücken, wie sehr die Königin die Bereitwilligkeit anerkannt mit welcher Sie ihrem Rufe gefolgt und unter die Waffen getreten sind.

Ich lebe der festen Ueberzeugung, dass Sie unter allen Umständen die Ehre einer Fahne aufrecht erhalten werden, die bis jetzt siegenreich in allen Theilen der Welt geweht hat, im Kampfen für Recht, Ordnung, und Freiheit, und zur Verbreitung der Civilisation.

Möge der Allmächtige Sie mit seinem Schutze in allen den Mühsalen und Gefahren begleiten, die Sie sich muthig entschlossen haben, mit der tapferen Englischen Armee zu theilen!

Sie wird Sie, daran zweifle ich nicht, als Brüder bewillkommen.

AT THE OPENING OF

THE GOLDEN-LANE SCHOOLS.

[MARCH 19TH, 1857.]

MR. ROGERS AND GENTLEMEN, PROMOTERS AND
SUPPORTERS OF THESE SCHOOLS,—

I THANK you heartily for your kind and
cordial welcome. I rejoice at the opportunity which has this day been afforded to me of
visiting this noble establishment, and my satisfaction in doing so is increased by the circumstance that my visit occurs at a period of its
existence when the state of useful development
to which by your exertions it has attained is
about, by a continuance of the same exertions, to
receive a still wider extension. In the progress
of these schools, struggling, I may say, from
the most lowly and humble beginnings up to
their present noble dimensions, we find a striking
exemplification of the Divine truth, that the
principle of good once sown is not destined
to lie dormant, but that, like the grain of

N 2

mustard-seed, it is calculated to extend and
develop itself in an ever-increasing sphere of
usefulness; and we may confidently hope that
what you have now effected, following this
universal law, will not be limited in its results to
the immediate objects of your charitable exertions,
but that it will prove the means of diffusing un-
told blessings among the most remote generations.
For you, Mr. Rogers, who have been mainly
instrumental, and at great personal sacrifice, in
bringing about this great good, and for those who
have stood by you, and contributed by their
support to the success of your efforts, there can,
I am sure, be no higher source of gratification
than in the contemplation of your own work.
The reflection that you have been the instrument,
under Divine Providence, of conferring upon the
poor and needy in this vast district that greatest
of all boons, the means of obtaining for their
children the blessings of education and of religious
instruction, without which any lasting success in
life or any permanent amelioration of their lot
would seem hopeless; and still further, the feeling that this inestimable blessing will be secured
in a yet higher degree to their children's children,
will carry with it its own best reward. Still it
will be a source of legitimate pride and satis-

faction to you to know that your labours have
not been unobserved, but that your noble and
Christianlike exertions to benefit those who cannot help themselves have attracted the notice
and admiration of your Sovereign, and of those
who are deputed under her to watch over and
promote the education and moral welfare of her
people. The means which you have adopted to
effect your work of benevolence appear no less
deserving of commendation than the object itself.
You have not been content with the bare attempt
to force, perhaps upon unwilling recipients, a
boon, the value of which might not be appreciated, but you have wisely sought to work upon
the convictions of the parents of the children you
wish to benefit by extending your assistance to
those who, by a small contribution out of their
hardly-won earnings, have proved that they are
awake to a sense of the vast importance it is to
their offspring that the means of being fitted to
pass successfully through life, and by honest
industry to better their worldly condition, should
be brought within their reach. It is a source of
high personal gratification to me that I have been
enabled, by my presence here this day, and by
that of the Prince of Wales, to mark, not only
my own appreciation of your labours, but also

the deep interest which the Queen takes in the well-being of the poorest of her subjects; and that gratification will be greatly enhanced if by this public expression of the sympathy of the Queen and of her family and Government this noble cause shall be still further advanced. Most earnestly do I pray that the same success which has hitherto blessed your labours may continue to attend your future progress, and that your example may stimulate other localities to emulate your useful efforts.

AT THE OPENING OF

THE EXHIBITION OF ART TREASURES

OF THE UNITED KINGDOM AT MANCHESTER.

[MAY 5TH, 1857.]

[The MAYOR of MANCHESTER having presented an Address,

His ROYAL HIGHNESS returned the following reply—]

MR. MAYOR, ALDERMEN, AND GENTLEMEN,—

I HAVE received with feelings of no ordinary gratification the address which you have presented to me, expressing such kindly feelings towards myself, and professing to represent the good wishes of the vast community which is collected in and around this city.

It will, I am sure, be most pleasing to the Queen to receive, from the expressions contained in the address, a fresh assurance of the loyal interest taken by her people in all that concerns her happiness.

I most willingly attend here this day to assist at a ceremony which the inhabitants of Manchester may well witness with pride, as its object is to inaugurate an Exhibition collected by the exertion of their enterprise and public spirit, and intended, not for the amusement and gratification of the neighbourhood alone, but for the instruction and improvement of the nation at large.

You justly allude in terms of gratitude to that comprehensive and liberal spirit which has adorned the walls of this building with the choicest specimens of art from so many private galleries of the kingdom. It added much to the pleasure with which the Queen and myself had complied with the application for works of art belonging to us when we found this example so generally followed by the possessors of treasures which are, in general, so reluctantly intrusted by their owners to the care of others.

The Queen will, I am confident, be glad again to visit Manchester, not only to mark by her presence her approval of the object and successful execution of this great undertaking which we have this day to celebrate, but from a recollection of the enthusiastic loyalty exhibited when she had formerly an opportunity of visiting this great centre of industry.

[Lord OVERSTONE having read the Address of the General Council,

His ROYAL HIGHNESS replied as follows—]

MY LORD AND GENTLEMEN,—

YOU are very kind in thinking at this moment of the bereavement which has befallen the Queen and her family.

In the Duchess of Gloucester we have all lost, not only the last of the children of that good King who occupied the throne during sixty years, and carried this country fearlessly and successfully through the most momentous struggles of its history, and thus the last personal link with those times, but also a lady whose virtues and qualities of the heart had commanded the respect and love of all who knew her.

If I have thought it my duty to attend here to-day, although her mortal remains have not yet been carried to their last place of rest, my decision has been rendered easy by the conviction that, could her own opinions and wishes have been known, she would, with that sense of duty and patriotic feeling which so much distinguished her and the generation to which she belonged, have been anxious that I should not on her account, or from private feelings, disturb an arrangement intended for the public good.

[Mr. FAIRBAIRN having presented the Address of the Executive Committee,

His ROYAL HIGHNESS returned the following reply—]

GENTLEMEN OF THE EXECUTIVE COMMITTEE,—

I THANK you most sincerely for your kind address.

The expressions of loyalty and attachment to

the Queen which it conveys will, I feel certain, be most gratifying to her.

I have with pleasure accepted your invitation to preside at the inaugural ceremony of an undertaking which I have watched with the deepest interest from its first conception ; and I may now be allowed to congratulate you upon the success which has so far crowned your labours.

The building in which we are assembled, and the wonderful collection of those treasures of art, as you so justly term them, which it displays, reflect the highest credit upon you. They must strike the beholder with grateful admiration, not only of the wealth and spirit of enterprise of this country, but also of that generous feeling of mutual confidence and goodwill between the different classes of society within it, of which it affords so gratifying a proof.

We behold a feast which the rich, and they who have, set before those to whom fortune has denied the higher luxuries of life—bringing forth from the innermost recesses of their private dwellings, and intrusting to your care, their choicest and most cherished treasures, in order to gratify the nation at large : and this, too, unhesitatingly, at your mere request, satisfied that your plans were disinterested and well

matured, and that they had the good of the
country for their object.

This is a gratifying sight, and blessed is the
country in which it is witnessed. But not less
so is the fact which has shown itself in this as in
other instances, that the great and noble of the
land look to their Sovereign to head and lead
them in such patriotic undertakings; and when
they see that the Sovereign has come forward to
give her countenance and assistance to the work,
that they feel it a pleasure to co-operate with
her and not to leave her without their support—
emulating thus, in works of peace, the chivalric
spirit which animated their forefathers in the
warlike times of old.

You have done well not to aim at a mere
accumulation of works of art and objects of
general interest, but to give to your collection,
by a scientific and historical arrangement, an
educational character,—thus not losing the opportunity of teaching the mind, as well as
gratifying the senses. And manifold are the
lessons which it will present to us! If art is
the purest expression of the state of mental and
religious culture, and of general civilization, of
any age or people, an historical and chronological
review given at one glance cannot fail to impress

us with a just appreciation of the peculiar characteristics of the different periods and countries
the works of which are here exhibited to us, and
of the influence which they have exercised upon
each other.

In comparing these works with those of our
own age and country, while we may well be
proud of the immense development of knowledge
and power of production which we possess, we
have reason also for humility in contemplating
the refinement of feeling and intensity of thought
manifested in the works of the older schools.

I trust that you may reap, in the approbation
of the public at large, and in the remunerative
concourse of the people, the immediate reward of
your labours; and that, like the Exhibition of
1851, to which you so flatteringly allude, you
may thus also find the means of closing your
operations without having recourse to the
Guarantee Fund which this district has so
generously put at your disposal.

Beyond this, however, I trust that the beneficial
effects upon the progress of art and taste in our
country; which we may confidently look to, may
be a lasting memorial of your vast enterprise.

CONFERENCE ON NATIONAL EDUCATION.

[JUNE 22ND, 1857.]

GENTLEMEN,—

WE have met to-day in the sacred cause of Education—of National Education. This word, which means no less than the moral and intellectual development of the rising generation, and, therefore, the national welfare, is well calculated to engross our minds, and opens a question worthy of a nation's deepest interest and most anxious consideration. Gentlemen, the nation is alive to its importance, and our presence here to-day gives further evidence (if such evidence were needed) of its anxiety to give it that consideration. Looking to former times, we find that our forefathers, with their wonted piety and paternal care, had established a system of national education, based upon the parish organization, and forming part of parish life, which met the wants of their day, and had

in it a certain unity and completeness which we
may well envy at the present moment. But in
the progress of time our wants have outstripped
that system, and the condition of the country
has so completely changed, even within these
last fifty years, that the old parochial division is
no longer adequate for the present population.
This has increased during that period in England and Wales from, in round numbers,
9,000,000 to 18,000,000, and, where there formerly existed comparatively small towns and
villages, we now see mighty cities, like Liver-
pool, Manchester, Hull, Leeds, Birmingham, and
others, with their hundreds of thousands, spring-
ing up almost, as it were, by enchantment;
London having increased to nearly two and a
half million of souls, and the factory district of
Lancashire alone having aggregated a population of nearly 3,000,000 within a radius of thirty
miles. This change could not escape the watchful eye of a patriotic public ; but how to provide
the means of satisfying the new wants could not
be a matter of easy solution. While zeal for the
public good, a fervent religious spirit, and true
philanthropy are qualities eminently distinguishing our countrymen, the love of liberty, and an
aversion from being controlled by the power of

the State in matters nearest to their hearts, are feelings which will always most powerfully influence them in action. Thus the common object has been contemplated from the most different points of view, and pursued often upon antagonistic principles. Some have sought the aid of Government, others that of the Church to which they belong; some have declared it to be the duty of the State to provide elementary instruction for the people at large, others have seen in the State interference a check to the spontaneous exertions of the people themselves, and an interference with self-government; some, again, have advocated a plan of compulsory education based upon local self-government, and others the voluntary system in its widest development. While these have been some of the political subjects of difference, those in the religious field have not been less marked and potent. We find, on the one hand, the wish to see secular and religious instruction separated, and the former recognized as an innate and inherent right, to which each member of society has a claim, and which ought not to be denied to him if he refuses to take along with it the inculcation of a particular dogma to which he objects as unsound; while we see, on the other hand, the doctrine asserted, that no education can be sound which does not rest on religious instruction, and that religious truth is too sacred to be modified and tampered with, even in its minutest deductions, for the sake of procuring a general agreement.

Gentlemen, if these differences were to have been discussed here to-day, I should not have been able to respond to your invitation to take the chair, as I should have thought it inconsistent with the position which I occupy, and with the duty which I owe to the Queen and the country at large. I see those here before me who have taken a leading part in these important discussions, and I am happy to meet them upon a neutral ground; happy to find that there *is* a neutral ground upon which their varied talents and abilities can be brought to bear in communion upon the common object; and proud and grateful to them that they should have allowed me to preside over them for the purpose of working together in the common vineyard. I feel certain that the greatest benefit must arise to the cause we have all so much at heart by the mere free exchange of your thoughts and various experience. You may well be proud, gentlemen, of the results hitherto achieved by your rival efforts, and may point to the fact that, since the beginning of the century, while the population has doubled itself, the number of schools, both public and private, has been multiplied fourteen times. In 1801 there were in England and Wales, of public schools, 2876; of private schools, 487—total, 3363. In 1851 (the year of the census) there were in England and Wales, of public schools, 15,518; of private schools, 30,524—total, 46,042; giving instruction in all to 2,144,378 scholars; of whom 1,422,982 belong to public schools, and 721,396 to the private schools. The rate of progress is further illustrated by statistics which show that in 1818 the proportion of day-scholars to the population was 1 in 17; in 1833, 1 in 11; and in 1851, 1 in 8. These are great results, although I hope they may only be received as instalments of what has yet to be done. But what must be your feelings when you reflect upon the fact, the inquiry into which has brought us together, that this great boon thus obtained for the mass of the people, and which is freely offered to them, should have been only partially accepted, and, upon the whole, so insufficiently applied as to render its use almost valueless! We are told that, the total population in England and Wales of children between the ages of 3 and 15 being estimated at 4,908,696, only

o

2,046,848 attend school at all, while 2,861,848
receive no instruction whatever. At the same
time an analysis of the scholars with reference to
the length of time allowed for their school tuition,
shows that 42 per cent. of them have been at
school for less than one year, 22 per cent. during
one year, 15 per cent. during two years, 9 per cent.
during three years, 5 per cent. during four years,
and 4 per cent. during five years. Therefore,
out of the two millions of scholars alluded to, more
than one million and a half remain only two
years at school. I leave it to you to judge what
the results of such an education can be. I find
further that of these two millions of children
attending school only about 600,000 are above
the age of nine.

Gentlemen, these are startling facts, which
render it evident that no extension of the means
of education will be of any avail unless this evil,
which lies at the root of the whole question, be
removed, and that it is high time that the
country should become thoroughly awake to its
existence, and prepared to meet it energetically.
To impress this upon the public mind is the
object of our conference. Public opinion is the
powerful lever which in these days moves a
people for good and for evil, and to public

opinion we must therefore appeal if we would achieve any lasting and beneficial results. You, gentlemen, will richly add to the services which you have already rendered to the noble cause if you will prepare public opinion by your inquiry into this state of things, and by discussing in your sections the causes of it as well as the remedies which may lie within our reach. This will be no easy matter; but even if your labours should not result in the adoption of any immediate practical steps, you will have done great good in preparing for them. It will probably happen that, in this instance as in most others, the cause which produces the evil will be more easily detected than its remedy, and yet a just appreciation of the former must ever be the first and essential condition for the discovery of the latter. You will probably trace the cause of our social condition to a state of ignorance and lethargic indifference on the subject among parents generally; but the root of the evil will, I suspect, be found to extend into that field on which the political economist exercises his activity—I mean the labour market— demand and supply. To dissipate that ignorance and rouse from that lethargy may be difficult; but with the united and earnest efforts of all who are the friends of the working classes it ought, after all, to be only a question of time. What measures can be brought to bear upon the other root of the evil is a more delicate question, and will require the nicest care in handling, for there you cut into the very quick of the working man's condition. His children are not only his offspring, to be reared for a future independent position, but they constitute part of his productive power, and work with him for the staff of life; the daughters especially are the handmaids of the house, the assistants of the mother, the nurses of the younger children, the aged, and the sick. To deprive the labouring family of their help would be almost to paralyse its domestic existence. On the other hand, carefully collected statistics reveal to us the fact, that, while about 600,000 children between the ages of 3 and 15 are absent from school, but known to be employed, no less than 2,200,000 are not at schools, whose absence cannot be traced to any ascertained employment or other legitimate cause. You will have to work, then, upon the minds and hearts of the parents, to place before them the irreparable mischief which they inflict upon those who are intrusted to their care by keeping them from the light of knowledge, to

bring home to their conviction that it is their
duty to exert themselves for their children's
education, bearing in mind at the same time
that it is not only their most sacred duty, but
also their highest privilege. Unless they work
with you, your work, our work, will be vain;
but you will not fail, I feel sure, in obtaining
their co-operation if you remind them of their
duty to their God and Creator. Our Heavenly
Father, in His boundless goodness, has made His
creatures that they should be happy, and in His
wisdom has fitted His means to His ends, giving
to all of them different qualities and faculties, in
using and developing which they fulfil their
destiny, and, running their uniform course according to His prescription, they find that happiness which He has intended for them. Man
alone is born into this world with faculties far
nobler than the other creatures, reflecting the
image of Him who has willed that there should
be beings on earth to know and worship Him,
but endowed with the power of self-determination, having reason given him for his guide.
He can develop his faculties, place himself in
harmony with his Divine prototype, and attain
that happiness which is offered to him on earth,
to be completed hereafter in entire union with

Him through the mercy of Christ. But he can also leave these faculties unimproved, and miss his mission on earth. He will then sink to the level of the lower animals, forfeit happiness, and separate from his God, whom he did know how to find. Gentlemen, I say man has no right to do this—he has no right to throw off the task which is laid upon him for his happiness; it is his duty to fulfil his mission to the utmost of his power; but it is our duty, the duty of those whom Providence has removed from this awful struggle and placed beyond this fearful danger, manfully, unceasingly, and untiringly to aid by advice, assistance, and example the great bulk of the people, who, without such aid, must almost inevitably succumb to the difficulty of their task. They will not cast from them the aiding hand, and the Almighty will bless the labours of those who work in His cause.

OPENING ADDRESS

AT THE

MEETING IN THE COLLEGE OF PHYSICIANS

FOR THE

INAUGURATION OF JENNER'S STATUE.

[MAY 17TH, 1858.]

———

1.

GENTLEMEN,—

YOU have invited me to take the chair at this meeting, convened on the anniversary of Jenner's birth for the purpose of doing honour to his memory ; and I have not hesitated to comply with your request, in order to mark, in common with you, my sense of the inestimable boon which this great philosopher and philanthropist has bestowed upon the human race.

His discovery was not the result of accident, like many others, however important, but that of long and thoughtful observation and reflection, and of continuous induction from numerous

facts and carefully conducted experiments, to
which a whole life had been directed. He has
thus been enabled to save by his discovery more
human lives than has fallen to the lot of any
other man, and England has just reason to be
proud to number him amongst her sons. Whilst
his contemporaries testify their feeling of gratitude to him by several important public acts, it
has been reserved to us to prove that we do not
less highly appreciate his services, by raising a
statue to his memory.   May it be long preserved
to exhibit the features of this benefactor of mankind to succeeding generations!

2.

I return you my best thanks for the kind
words which you have spoken, and assure you
that I shall feel most happy if the result of this
day's meeting should be to rouse afresh public
attention to the means of safety which science
has placed at man's command, and the neglect of
which still costs this country alone no less than
annually 5000 victims.

AT THE TRINITY HOUSE.

[JULY 3RD, 1858.]

1.

" THE QUEEN."

MAY she long continue in the possession of that great blessing, " The love of her " people ! "

2.

I have to propose to you the Health of " The " Prince of Wales," and the rest of the " Royal " Family."

Since I last met you here, it has pleased the Almighty to take the last of the children of King George the Third from amongst us, in the beloved and revered Duchess of Gloucester; another daughter has been vouchsafed to the Queen ; and our eldest child has, united to a husband of her choice—and, I may say, worthy of her choice— passed to a distant country, where I was happy

to find her the other day in the possession of
every domestic blessing. The interest and sympathy evinced by the people of this country in
this marriage could not but be most gratifying
to the feelings of her parents.

3.

The toast which I now propose to you is the
" Army and Navy."

If this toast must at all times be received
by Englishmen with feelings of pride and satisfaction, who could approach it at the present
moment without being also penetrated by those
of admiration and deep thankfulness for the
heroic deeds and sacrifices with which our
gallant troops are now struggling, not only for
the honour and interests of our country, but I
trust for the cause of civilization and the future
happiness of millions of people now unfortunately
in part our enemies ! May the Almighty continue to watch over our brave countrymen in
the East, and grant them uninterrupted victory !
His hand becomes most apparent when we consider how small are the means with which so
much has been achieved. The deepest responsibility, however, attaches to us, not to rest satis-

fied with the enjoyment of the advantages and successes obtained by such self-sacrificing devotion, but to take care that, by maintaining these noble services in sufficient numbers, the tasks which for our benefit may be from time to time imposed upon them, should not carry with them the almost certain immolation of those who are expected to perform them.

6.

I propose to you " the Health of Her Majesty's " Ministers and the Earl of Derby."

They are called upon to administer and advise the Sovereign upon the multifarious and complicated affairs of this vast empire. In these days, moreover, when the progress of education and civilization renders the influence of public opinion upon the conduct of the Government more and more powerful, the latter has this difficult problem to solve : it has to maintain a judicious and beneficial harmony between its own conscientious convictions, and the impulsive and varying character of that public opinion.

If I might in this room be allowed to make use of a nautical metaphor, I should compare the governing body with a vessel, of which

public opinion is the rudder. Should their
nautical action not be most nicely adjusted, one
of two results must follow—either the vessel
would refuse to answer her helm, and to take
the desired course; or she would answer it too
quickly, which I believe you call wild steering,
the effects of which may be seen in the zigzag
line of the wake.

Nothing, however, can tend more to facilitate
the difficult task of the Government, than that
their motives and intentions should be understood and appreciated by their fellow-countrymen; and it is on occasions like the present that
these can testify those feelings. With this view
I now ask you to drink to the " Health of Her
" Majesty's Ministers."

N.B.—Nos. 4 and 5 were answers to " My
" Health," and " Prosperity to the Trinity
" House." I read extracts of Reports on all
business connected with the Corporation.

SPEECH DELIVERED AT CHERBOURG

AFTER THE

BANQUET ON BOARD " LA BRETAGNE."

[AUGUST 5TH, 1858.]

———

LA Reine désire que j'exprime à Votre Majesté combien elle est sensible à la nouvelle preuve d'amitié que vous venez de lui donner, en lui portant une toast, et en prononçant des paroles qui lui resteront chères à jamais.

Votre Majesté connait les sentiments d'amitié qu'elle vous porte, à vous, Sire, et à l'Impératrice, et je n'ai pas besoin de vous les rappeler. Vous savez également que la bonne entente entre nos deux pays est l'objet constant de ses désirs, comme il l'est des vôtres. La Reine est donc doublement heureuse d'avoir l'occasion, par sa présence ici en ce moment, de s'allier à vous, Sire, en tâchant de reserrer, autant que possible, les liens d'amitié entre les deux peuples. Cette amitié est la base de leur prospérité mutuelle, et la bénédiction du Ciel ne lui manquera pas !

La Reine porte la santé de l'Empereur et de l'Impératrice !

ON PRESENTING NEW COLOURS

TO THE

2ND BATTALION OF THE 13TH (" PRINCE ALBERT'S OWN ") LIGHT INFANTRY,

AT HARFORD RIDGE, NEAR ALDERSHOT.

[FEBRUARY 21ST, 1859.]

THE act which has just been performed, simple as it is, has the highest significance for the soldier! You have received in these colours the emblems of your country and your Sovereign, and of your regiment as a part of the British Army. It is your country's, your Sovereign's, and that army's honour which is bound up in them, and which you will henceforth have to guard and to defend; not by your valour alone in action, and your endurance under the hardships of campaigns, but also during the monotonous duties of peace and under the temptations of inaction—placed in different societies, under different climes, and in different parts of the world.

The British soldier has to follow these colours
to every part of the globe, and everywhere he is
the representative of his country's power, freedom,
loyalty, and civilization. The 13th has a fair
name in the world, won chiefly in distant lands—
the West Indies, America, Africa, and Asia ;
and its defence of Jellalabad has proved that
it is capable of evincing the highest qualities of
the soldier. You may point with just pride to
the fact that those qualities, displayed so con-
spicuously under Sir Robert Sale, were but now
exhibited to the admiration of mankind by Sir
Henry Havelock, an officer trained in its ranks !

You are a new, a young battalion, sprung
with surprising rapidity together with others
from a patriotic people, for the rescue of the
country's mightiest interests threatened in the
East. During the short time you have been
together you have worked hard to assume the
honourable position intrusted to you, and I may
now congratulate you on your success. That
the military authorities should think you fit and
worthy to take your place in the Army of the
Cape, shows that your exertions are appreciated
and that entire confidence is reposed in you.

I feel proud that you should bear my name to
that promising country.

May God's best blessing attend you, shield you from danger, support you under difficulties, cheer you under privations, grant you moderation in success, contentment under discipline, humility and gratitude towards Him in prosperity!

AT THE MEETING OF

THE BRITISH ASSOCIATION FOR THE ADVANCEMENT OF SCIENCE.

[HELD AT ABERDEEN, SEPTEMBER 14TH, 1859.]

GENTLEMEN OF THE BRITISH ASSOCIATION,—

YOUR kind invitation to me to undertake the office of your President for the ensuing year could not but startle me on its first announcement. The high position which Science occupies, the vast number of distinguished men who labour in her sacred cause, and whose achievements, while spreading innumerable benefits, justly attract the admiration of mankind, contrasted strongly in my mind with the consciousness of my own insignificance in this respect. I, a simple admirer, and would-be student of Science, to take the place of the chief and spokesman of the scientific men of the day, assembled in furtherance of their important objects!—the thing appeared to me impossible. Yet, on reflection, I came to the conclusion that,

P

if not as a contributor to, or director of your labours, I might still be useful to you, useful to science, by accepting your offer. Remembering that this Association is a popular Association, not a secret confraternity of men jealously guarding the mysteries of their profession, but inviting the uninitiated, the public at large, to join them, having as one of its objects to break down those imaginary and hurtful barriers which exist between men of science and so-called men of practice—I felt that I could, from the peculiar position in which Providence has placed me in this country, appear as the representative of that large public, which profits by and admires your exertions, but is unable actively to join in them; that my election was an act of humility on your part, which to reject would have looked like false humility, that is like pride, on mine. But I reflected further, and saw in my acceptance the means, of which necessarily so few are offered to Her Majesty, of testifying to you, through the instrumentality of her husband, that your labours are not unappreciated by your Sovereign, and that she wishes her people to know this as well as yourselves. Guided by these reflections, my choice was speedily made, for the path of duty lay straight before me.

If these, however, are the motives which have induced me to accept your flattering offer of the Presidency, a request on my part is hardly necessary that you will receive my efforts to fulfil its duties with kind indulgence.

If it were possible for anything to make me still more aware how much I stand in need of this indulgence, it is the recollection of the person whom I have to succeed as your President—a man of whom this country is justly proud, and whose name stands among the foremost of the naturalists in Europe for his patience in investigation, conscientiousness in observation, boldness of imagination, and acuteness in reasoning. You have no doubt listened with pleasure to his parting address, and I beg to thank him for the flattering manner in which he has alluded to me in it.

The Association meets for the first time to-day in these regions and in this ancient and interesting city. The poet, in his works of fiction, has to choose, and anxiously to weigh, where to lay his scene, knowing that, like the painter, he is thus laying in the background of his picture, which will give tone and colour to the whole. The stern and dry reality of life is governed by the same laws, and we are here living, feeling,

P 2

and thinking under the influence of the local impressions of this northern seaport. The choice appears to me a good one. The travelling philosophers have had to come far ; but in approaching the Highlands of Scotland they meet nature in its wild and primitive form, and nature is the object of their studies. The geologist will not find many novelties in yonder mountains, because he will stand there on the bare backbone of the globe ; but the primary rocks, which stand out in their nakedness, exhibit the grandeur and beauty of their peculiar form, and in the splendid quarries of this neighbourhood are seen to peculiar advantage the closeness and hardness of their mass, and their inexhaustible supply for the use of man, made available by the application of new mechanical powers. On this primitive soil the botanist and zoologist will be attracted only by a limited range of plants and animals ; but they are the very species which the extension of agriculture and increase of population are gradually driving out of many parts of the country. On those blue hills the red deer, in vast herds, holds undisturbed dominion over the wide heathery forest, until the sportsman, fatigued and unstrung by the busy life of the bustling town, invades

the moor, to regain health and vigour by mea-
suring his strength with that of the antlered
monarch of the hill. But, notwithstanding all
his efforts to overcome an antagonist possessed
of such superiority of power, swiftness, caution,
and keenness of all the senses, the sportsman
would find himself baffled, had not science
supplied him the telescope and those terrible
weapons which seem daily to progress in the
precision with which they carry the deadly
bullet, mocking distance, to the mark.

In return for the help which Science has
afforded him, the sportsman can supply the
naturalist with many facts which he alone has
opportunity of observing, and which may assist
the solution of some interesting problems suggested by the life of the deer. Man also, the
highest object of our study, is found in vigorous,
healthy development, presenting a happy mix-
ture of the Celt, Goth, Saxon, and Dane, acquiring his strength on the hills and the sea. The
Aberdeen whaler braves the icy regions of the
Polar Sea, to seek and to battle with the great
monster of the deep : he has materially assisted
in opening these icebound regions to the researches of Science ; he fearlessly aided in the
search after Sir John Franklin and his gallant

companions, whom their country sent forth on this mission, but to whom Providence, alas! has denied the reward of their labours, the return to their homes, to the affectionate embrace of their families and friends, and the acknowledgments of a grateful nation. The city of Aberdeen itself is rich in interest for the philosopher. Its two lately united Universities make it a seat of learning and science. The collection of antiquities, formed for the present occasion, enables him to dive into olden times, and, by contact with the remains of the handiworks of the ancient inhabitants of Scotland, to enter into the spirit of that peculiar and interesting people, which has always attracted the attention and touched the hearts of men accessible to the influence of heroic poetry. The Spalding Club, founded in this city for the preservation of the historical and literary remains of the north-eastern counties of Scotland, is honourably known by its important publications.

Gentlemen!—This is the twenty-ninth anniversary of the foundation of this Association; and well may we look back with satisfaction to its operation and achievements throughout the time of its existence. When, on the 27th of September, 1831, the meeting of the Yorkshire

Philosophical Society took place at York, in the theatre of the Yorkshire Museum, under the presidency of the late Earl Fitzwilliam, then Viscount Milton, and the Rev. W. Vernon Harcourt eloquently set forth the plan for the formation of a British Association for the Promotion of Science, which he showed to have become a want for his country, the most ardent supporter of this resolution could not have anticipated that it would start into life full-grown as it were, enter at once upon its career of usefulness, and pursue it without deviation from the original design, triumphing over the oppositions which it had to encounter in common with everything that is new and claims to be useful. Gentlemen, this proved that the want was a real, and not an imaginary one, and that the mode in which it was intended to supply that want was based upon a just appreciation of unalterable truths. Mr. Vernon Harcourt summed up the desiderata in graphic words, which have almost identically been retained as the exposition of the objects of the Society, printed at the head of the annually-appearing volume of its Transactions:—" to give a stronger " impulse and more systematic direction to " scientific inquiry—to promote the intercourse

" of those who cultivate Science in different
" parts of the empire, with one another and
" with foreign philosophers—and to obtain a
" more general attention to the objects of
" Science, and a removal of any disadvantages
" of a public kind which impede its progress."

To define the nature of Science, to give an
exact and complete definition of what that
Science, to whose service the Association is
devoted, is and means, has, as it naturally must,
at all times occupied the Metaphysician. He
has answered the question in various ways,
more or less satisfactorily to himself or others.
To me, Science, in its most general and comprehensive acceptation, means the knowledge of
what I know, the consciousness of human knowledge. Hence, to know is the object of all
Science ; and all special knowledge, if brought
to our consciousness in its separate distinctive-
ness from, and yet in its recognized relation to
the totality of our knowledge, is scientific knowledge. We require, then, for Science—that is
to say, for the acquisition of scientific knowledge—those two activities of our mind which
are necessary for the acquisition of *any* knowledge — analysis and synthesis ; the first, to
dissect and reduce into its component parts the

object to be investigated, and to render an accurate account to ourselves of the nature and qualities of these parts by observation; the second to recompose the observed and understood parts into a unity in our consciousness, exactly answering to the object of our investigation. The labours of the man of Science are therefore at once the most humble and the loftiest which man can undertake. He only does what every little child does from its first awakening into life, and must do every moment of its existence; and yet he aims at the gradual approximation to divine truth itself. If, then, there exists no difference between the work of the man of Science and that of the merest child, what constitutes the distinction? Merely the conscious self-determination. The child observes what accident brings before it, and unconsciously forms its notion of it; the so-called practical man observes what his special work forces upon him, and he forms his notions upon it with reference to this particular work. The man of Science observes what he intends to observe, and knows why he intends it. The value which the peculiar object has in his eyes is not determined by accident, nor by an external cause, such as the mere connection with work to be performed, but by the place which he knows this object to hold in the general universe of knowledge, by the relation which it bears to other parts of that general knowledge.

To *arrange* and *classify* that universe of knowledge becomes therefore the first, and perhaps the most important, object and duty of Science. It is only when brought into a system, by separating the incongruous and combining those elements in which we have been enabled to discover the internal connection which the Almighty has implanted in them, that we can hope to grapple with the boundlessness of His creation, and with the laws which govern both mind and matter.

The operation of Science then has been, systematically to divide human knowledge, and raise, as it were, the separate groups of subjects for scientific consideration, into different and distinct sciences. The tendency to create new sciences is peculiarly apparent in our present age, and is perhaps inseparable from so rapid a progress as we have seen in our days; for the acquaintance with and mastering of distinct branches of knowledge enables the eye, from the newly gained points of sight, to see the new ramifications into which they divide themselves in strict consecutiveness and with logical necessity. But in thus gaining new centres of light, from which to direct our researches, and new and powerful means of adding to its ever-increasing treasures, Science approaches no nearer to the limits of its range, although travelling further and further from its original point of departure. For God's world is infinite; and the boundlessness of the universe, whose confines appear ever to retreat before our finite minds, strikes us no less with awe when, prying into the starry crowd of heaven, we find new worlds revealed to us by every increase in the power of the telescope, than when the microscope discloses to us in a drop of water, or an atom of dust, new worlds of life and animation, or the remains of such as have passed away.

Whilst the tendency to push systematic investigation in every direction enables the individual mind of man to bring all the power of which he is capable to bear on the specialities of his study, and enables a greater number of labourers to take part in the universal work, it may be feared that that consciousness of its unity which must pervade the whole of Science if it is not to lose its last and highest point of sight, may suffer. It has occasionally been given to rare intellects and the highest genius to follow the various sciences in their divergent roads, and yet to preserve that point of sight from which alone their totality can be contemplated and directed. Yet how rare is the appearance of such gifted intellects ! and if they be found at intervals, they remain still single individuals, with all the imperfections of human nature.

The only mode of supplying with any certainty this want, is to be sought in the combination of men of Science representing all the specialities, and working together for the common object of preserving that unity and presiding over that general direction. This has been to some extent done in many countries by the establishment of academies embracing the whole range of the sciences, whether physical or metaphysical, historical or political. In the absence of such an institution in this country, all lovers of Science must rejoice at the existence and activity of this Association, which embraces in its sphere of action, if not the whole range of the sciences, yet a very large and important section of them, those known as the *inductive sciences*, excluding all that are not approached by the inductive method of investigation. It has, for instance (and, considering its peculiar organization and mode of action, perhaps not unwisely), eliminated from its consideration and discussions those which come under the description of moral and political sciences. This has not been done from undervaluing their importance and denying their sacred right to the special attention of mankind, but from a desire to deal with those subjects only which can be reduced to positive proof, and do not rest on opinion or faith. The subjects of the moral and political sciences involve not only opinions but feelings; and their discussion frequently rouses passions. For feelings are " subjective," as the German metaphysician has it—they are inseparable from the individual being—an âttack upon them is felt as one upon the person itself; whilst facts are " objective " and belong to everybody—they remain the same facts at all times and under all circumstances : they can be proved; they have to be proved, and, when proved, are finally settled. It is with facts only that the Association deals. There may for a time exist differences of opinion on these also, but the process of removing them and resolving them into agreement is a different one from that in the moral and political sciences. These are generally approached by the *deductive* process; but if the reasoning be ever so acute and logically correct, and the point of departure, which may be arbitrarily selected, is disputed, no agreement is possible ; whilst we proceed here by the *inductive* process, taking nothing on trust, nothing for granted, but reasoning upwards from the meanest fact established, and making every step sure before going one beyond it, like the engineer in his approaches to a fortress. We thus gain ultimately a roadway, a ladder by which even a child may, almost without knowing it, ascend to the summit of truth and obtain that immensely wide and extensive view which is spread below the feet of the astonished beholder. This road has been shown us by the great Bacon ; and who can contemplate the prospects which it opens, without almost falling into a trance similar to that in which he allowed his imagination to wander over future ages of discovery !

From amongst the political sciences it has been attempted in modern times to detach one which admits of being severed from individual political opinions, and of being reduced to abstract laws derived from well-authenticated facts. I mean Political Economy, based on general statistics. A new Association has recently been formed, imitating our perambulating habits, and striving to comprehend in its investigations and discussions even a still more extended range of subjects, in what is called "Social Science." These efforts deserve our warmest approbation and good will. May they succeed in obtaining a purely and strictly scientific character! Our own Association has, since its meeting at Dublin, recognized the growing claims of Political Economy to scientific brotherhood, and admitted it into its Statistical Section. It could not have done so under abler guidance and happier auspices than the presidency of the Archbishop of Dublin, Dr. Whately, whose efforts in this direction are so universally appreciated. But even in this section, and whilst statistics alone were treated in it, the Association as far back as 1833 made it a rule that, in order to ensure positive results, only those classes of facts should be admitted which were capable of being expressed by numbers, and which promised, when sufficiently multiplied, to indicate general laws.

If, then, the main object of Science—and I beg to be understood, henceforth, as speaking only of that section which the Association has under its special care, viz. Inductive Science—if, I say, the object of Science is the discovery of the laws which govern natural phænomena, the primary condition for its success is : accurate observation and collection of facts in such comprehensiveness and completeness as to furnish the philosopher with the necessary material from which to draw safe conclusions.

Science is not of yesterday. We stand on the shoulders of past ages, and the amount of observations made, and facts ascertained, has been transmitted to us and carefully preserved in the various storehouses of Science ; other crops have been reaped, but still lie scattered on the field ; many a rich harvest is ripe for cutting, but waits for the reaper. Economy of labour is the essence of good husbandry, and no less so in the field of Science. Our Association has felt the importance of this truth, and may well claim, as one of its principal merits, the constant endeavour to secure that economy.

One of the latest undertakings of the Association has been, in conjunction with the Royal Society, to attempt the compilation of a classified catalogue of scientific memoirs, which, by combining under one head the titles of all memoirs written on a certain subject, will, when completed, enable the student who wishes to gain information on that subject to do so with the

greatest ease. It gives him, as it were, the plan
of the house, and the key to the different apart-
ments in which the treasures relating to his
subject are stored, saving him at once a painful
and laborious search, and affording him at the
same time an assurance that what is here offered
contains the whole of the treasures yet acquired.

While this has been one of its latest attempts,
the Association has from its very beginning kept
in view that its main sphere of usefulness lay in
that concentrated attention to all scientific operations which a general gives to the movements of
his army, watching and regulating the progress
of his impetuous soldiers in the different directions to which their ardour may have led them,
carefully noting the gaps which may arise from
their independent and eccentric action, and
attentively observing what impediments may
have stopped, or may threaten to stop, the progress of certain columns.

Thus it attempts to fix and record the position
and progress of the different labours, by its
Reports on the state of Sciences published
annually in its Transactions;—thus it directs
the attention of the labourers to those gaps
which require to be filled up, if the progress is
to be a safe and steady one;—thus it comes for-

ward with a helping hand in striving to remove those impediments which the unaided efforts of the individual labourer have been or may be unable to overcome.

Let us follow the activity of the Association in these three different directions.

The Reports on the state of Science originate in the conviction of the necessity for fixing, at given intervals, with accuracy and completeness, the position at which it has arrived. For this object the General Committee of the Association intrusts to distinguished individuals in the different branches of Science the charge of becoming, as it were, the biographers of the period. There are special points in different Sciences in which it sometimes appears desirable to the different Sections to have special Reports elaborated ; in such cases the General Committee, in its capacity of the representative assembly of all the Sciences, reserves to itself the right of judging what may be of sufficient importance to be thus recorded.

The special subjects which the Association points out for investigation, in order to supply the gaps which it may have observed, are— either such as the philosopher alone can success-fully investigate, because they require the close

attention of a practised observer, and a thorough
knowledge of the particular subject; or they are
such as require the greatest possible number of
facts to be obtained. Here Science often stands
in need of the assistance of the general public,
and gratefully accepts any contributions offered,
provided the facts be accurately observed. In
either case the Association points out *what* is to
be observed, and *how* it is to be observed.

The first is the result of the same careful
sifting process which the Association employs in
directing the issue of special Reports. The investigations are intrusted to specially-appointed
committees, or selected individuals. They are
in most cases not unattended with considerable
expense, and the Association, not content with
merely suggesting and directing, furnishes by
special grants the pecuniary means for defraying
the outlay caused by the nature and extent of
the inquiry. If we consider that the income of
the Association is solely derived from the contributions of its members, the fact that no less a
sum than 17,000*l.* has, since its commencement,
been thus granted for scientific purposes, is
certainly most gratifying.

The question *how* to observe, resolves itself
into two—that of the scientific method which is

to be employed in approaching a problem or in making an observation, and that of the philosophical instruments used in the observation or experiment. The Association brings to bear the combined knowledge and experience of the scientific men, not only of this but of other countries, on the discovery of that method which, while it economizes time and labour, promises the most accurate results. The method to which, after careful examination, the palm has been awarded, is then placed at the free disposal and use of all scientific investigators. The Association also issues, where practicable, printed forms, merely requiring the different heads to be filled up, which, by their uniformity, become an important means for assisting the subsequent reduction of the observations for the abstraction of the laws which they may indicate.

At the same time most searching tests and inquiries are constantly carried on in the Observatory at Kew, given to the Association by Her Majesty, the object of which is practically to test the relative value of different methods and instruments, and to guide the constantly progressive improvements in the construction of the latter.

The establishment at Kew has undertaken the

further important service of verifying and cor-
recting to a fixed standard the instruments of
any maker, to enable observations made with
them to be reduced to the same numerical expression. I need hardly remind the inhabitants
of Aberdeen that the Association, in one of the
first years of its existence, undertook the comparative measurement of the Aberdeen standard
scale with that of Greenwich,—a research ably
carried out by the late Mr. Baily.

The impediments to the general progress of
Science, the removal of which I have indicated
as one of the tasks which the Association has set
for itself, are of various kinds. If they were
only such as direction, advice, and encouragement would enable the individual, or even
combined efforts of philosophers, to overcome,
the exertions of the Association which I have
just alluded to might be sufficient for the purpose. But they are often such as can only be
successfully dealt with by the powerful arm of
the State or the long purse of the nation.
These impediments may be caused either by the
social condition of the country itself, by restric-
tions arising out of peculiar laws, by the political
separation of different countries, or by the magnitude of the undertakings being out of all

proportion to the means and power of single
individuals, of the Association, or even the
voluntary efforts of the public. In these cases,
the Association, together with its sister society,
" The Royal Society," becomes the spokesman
of Science with the Crown, the Government, or
Parliament—sometimes even, through the Home
Government, with foreign Governments. Thus
it obtained the establishment, by the British
Government, of magnetic and meteorological
observatories in six different parts of the globe,
as the beginning of a network of stations which
we must hope will be so far extended as to com-
pass by their geographical distribution the whole
of the phenomena which throw light on this
important point in our tellurian and even cosmi-
cal existence. The Institute of France, at the
recommendation of M. Arago, whose loss the
scientific world must long deplore, cheerfully
co-operated with our Council on this occasion.
It was our Association which, in conjunction
with the Royal Society, suggested the Antarctic
Expedition, with a view to further the discovery
of the laws of terrestrial magnetism, and thus
led to the discovery of the southern polar continent. It urged on the Admiralty the prosecution
of the tidal observations, which that department

has since fully carried out.   It recommended the establishment, in the British Museum, of the conchological collection exhibiting present and extinct species, which has now become an object of the greatest interest.

I will not weary you by further examples, with which most of you are better acquainted than I am myself, but merely express my satisfaction that there should exist bodies of men who will bring the well-considered and understood wants of Science before the public and the Government, who will even hand round the begging-box and expose themselves to refusals and rebuffs to which all beggars are liable, with the certainty, besides, of being considered great bores.   Please to recollect that this species of bore is a most useful animal, well adapted for the ends for which Nature intended him.   He alone, by constantly returning to the charge, and repeating the same truths and the same requests, succeeds in awakening attention to the cause which he advocates, and obtains that hearing which is granted him at last for self-protection, as the minor evil compared to his importunity, but which is requisite to make his cause understood.   This is more particularly the case in a free, active, enterprizing, and self-determining people like ours, where every interest works for itself, considers itself the all-important one, and makes its way in the world by its own efforts. Is it, then, to be wondered at, that the interests of Science—abstract as Science appears, and not immediately showing a return in pounds, shillings, and pence—should be postponed, at least, to others which promise immediate tangible results? Is it to be wondered at, that even our public men require an effort to wean themselves from other subjects in order to give their attention to Science and men of Science, when it is remembered that Science, with the exception of mathematics, was until of late almost systematically excluded from our school and university education—that the traditions of early life are those which make and leave the strongest impression on the human mind, and that the subjects with which we become acquainted, and to which our energies are devoted in youth, are those for which we retain the liveliest interest in after years—and that for these reasons the effort required must be both a mental and a moral one? A deep debt of gratitude is therefore due to bodies like this Association, which not only urges the wants of Science on the Government, but furnishes it at once with well-matured plans how to supply them with the greatest certainty and to the greatest public advantage.

We may be justified in hoping, however, that by the gradual diffusion of Science, and its inreasing recognition as a principal part of our national education, the public in general, no less than the Legislature and the State, will more and more recognize the claims of Science to their attention ; so that it may no longer require the begging-box, but speak to the State like a favoured child to its parent, sure of his parental solicitude for its welfare ; that the State will recognize in Science one of its elements of strength and prosperity, to foster which the clearest dictates of self-interest demand.

If the activity of this Association, such as I have endeavoured to describe it, ever found or could find its personification in one individual— its incarnation as it were—this had been found in that distinguished and revered philosopher who has been removed from amongst us in his ninetieth year, within these last few months. Alexander von Humboldt incessantly strove after dominion over that universality of human knowledge which stands in need of thoughtful government and direction to preserve its integrity; he strove to tie up the *fasces* of scientific knowledge, to give them strength in unity. He treated all scientific men as members of one family, enthusiastically directing, fostering, and encouraging inquiry, where he saw either the want of, or the willingness for it. His protection of the young and ardent student led many to success in their pursuit. His personal influence with the Courts and Governments of most countries in Europe enabled him to plead the cause of Science in a manner which made it more difficult for them to refuse than to grant what he requested. All lovers of Science deeply mourn for the loss of such a man. Gentlemen, it is a singular coincidence, that this very day on which we are here assembled, and are thus giving expression to our admiration of him, should be the anniversary of his birth.

To return to ourselves, however : one part of the functions of the Association can receive no personal representation, no incarnation : I mean the very fact of meetings like that which we are at present inaugurating. This is not the thoughtful direction of one mind over acquired knowledge, but the production of new thought by the contact of many minds, as the spark is produced by the friction of flint and steel ; it is not the action of the monarchy of a paternal Government, but the republican activity of the Roman Forum. These meetings draw forth the philosopher from the hidden recesses of his study, call in the wanderer over the field of science to meet his brethren, to lay before them the results of his labours, to set forth the deductions at which he has arrived, to ask for their examination, to maintain in the combat of debate the truth of his positions and the accuracy of his observations. These meetings, unlike those of any other Society, throw open the arena to the cultivators of all sciences, to their mutual advantage : the geologist learns from the chemist that there are problems for which he had no clue, but which that science can solve for him ; the geographer receives light from the naturalist, the astronomer from the physicist and engineer, and so on. And all find a field upon which to meet the public at large,—invite them to listen to their reports and even to take part in their discussions,—show to them that philosophers are not vain theorists, but essentially men of practice —not conceited pedants, wrapped up in their own mysterious importance, but humble inquirers after truth, proud only of what they may have achieved or won for the general use of man.

Neither are they daring and presumptuous un-
believers—a character which ignorance has sometimes affixed to them—who would, like the
Titans, storm heaven by placing mountain upon
mountain, till hurled down from the height attained, by the terrible thunders of outraged Jove;
but rather the pious pilgrims to the Holy Land,
who toil on in search of the sacred shrine, in
search of truth—God's truth—God's laws as
manifested in His works, in His creation.

AT THE DINNER

ON THE

OPENING OF THE CLOTHWORKERS' HALL,

IN THE CITY.

[MARCH 27TH, 1860.]

SIR, AND GENTLEMEN,—

I BEG to return you my best thanks for your kindness in drinking my health with such gratifying demonstrations of good will towards me.

It is in accordance with our nature, that, after having accomplished a task and succeeded in any work of our hands, we should banish from our minds the recollection of the troubles and anxieties which accompanied its conception and progress, and rejoice not only ourselves in our success, but ask our neighbours and friends to come and rejoice with us. We want them to see what we have done, and to share in our satisfaction.

I am grateful to you that you should have thought of including me in the number of your friends, for I can, I assure you, fully appreciate your undertaking, and honestly congratulate you on your success.

It must have cost you some hesitation and regret to separate yourselves from a hall in which your forefathers had feasted the first Kings of the House of Stuart, and in which they, as well as yourselves, habitually met for business and re-creation. But the marks of man, like the organic bodies in nature, to be preserved require to be continually renewed, and thus alone resist the destructive tendency of time ; and you determined (as we see to-day) to follow Nature also in the law of increase, and to show that you have grown and expanded within these two hundred years. Your desire to see me amongst you upon this occasion, which I must attribute to your loyalty to the Queen, and my pleasure in responding to your call, proves, at the same time, that those feelings of mutual regard and affection which subsisted two hundred years ago between these great and wealthy companies, these little in-dependent republics of the City of London, and the Crown, have withstood the effects of time, are living, ay—and I trust are even grown in intensity and warmth. In such feelings we gladly recognize one of the essential conditions of the political and social life of a free and prosperous nation.

May these blessings be preserved to this favoured land from generation to generation! and may this Corporation, of which I feel proud to have by your kindness been admitted to-day as a member, live and prosper on, as one of the important links which connect succeeding generations with those which have long passed away!

Let me drink to the health of our Master and Wardens, and Prosperity to the " Clothworkers' " Company! "

AT THE

BANQUETING-ROOM, ST. JAMES'S PALACE,

ON THE OCCASION OF THE

200TH ANNIVERSARY OF THE FORMATION OF THE GRENADIER GUARDS.

[JUNE 16TH, 1860.]

GENTLEMEN,—

1.

"THE QUEEN."

2.

I AM much obliged to Colonel Lewis for the kind terms in which he has proposed to you to drink my health, and much gratified at the feelings which you have evinced by the manner in which you have responded to his proposal.

Gentlemen!—I was justly proud of the distinguished honour conferred upon me when I was appointed, eight years ago, to succeed the

immortal Duke of Wellington in the command
of this regiment, and of having since held this
honourable post, which connects me with you,
not only officially, but on terms of intimate and I
hope cordial personal relations; but it is on an
occasion like the present that the consideration
must rise to my mind in its full force,—what
honour and distinction is involved in the title of
Colonel of the Grenadier Guards.

We are assembled to celebrate the 200th
Anniversary of the formation of the Regiment
as at present constituted — 200 years, which
embrace the most glorious period of the history
of our country—and in the most glorious events
of this history the Regiment has borne an important and distinguished part. It has fought
at sea and on land, in most parts of Europe, in
Africa and America; and, whether fighting the
French, Dutch, Spaniards, Moors, Turks, or
Russians, it has stood to its colours, upheld the
honour of the British name, and powerfully
contributed to those successes which have, under
God's blessing, made that name stand proudly
forth amongst the nations of the earth.

I need not recall to your recollection its deeds,
which must be all present to your minds, but I
cannot forego on such an occasion pointing at

R

least to some of the most important of the long
and uninterrupted list of victories with which
the Grenadier Guards have been associated. I
must point to the celebrated siege and capture
of Namur, the first defence of Gibraltar, the
capture of Barcelona and Valencia, the battles
of Blenheim, Ramillies, Oudenarde, and Mal-
plaquet, the battle of Dettingen, ay! and of
Fontenoy, where, though the victory did not
ultimately remain with the Allies, it was fairly
won, as far as the English were concerned, and
that by the conspicuous prowess of the Grenadier Guards! the capture of Cherbourg, which,
just a century ago, looked grimly across at
our shores; the battles in Germany under the
Marquis of Granby; the battle of Lincelles;
those of Corunna, Barrosa, and the Pyrenees;
the capture of St. Sebastian; battles of Nive
and Nivelle, and of Waterloo, in which last
great struggle with Napoleon the Regiment
acquired the title of Grenadier Guards, from
having defeated, in fair fight, those noble and
devoted grenadiers of his Imperial Guard, who,
till met by the British bayonet, had been considered invincible; and more lately the battles
of the Alma and of Inkerman, and the long-
protracted siege of Sevastopol.

These are glorious annals, and proud the corps may well be which can show the like! But the duty of the soldier unfortunately is not confined to fighting the foreign enemies of his country, it has at times been his fate to have to stand in arms against even his own brothers! a mournful duty, which we may trust never to see again imposed upon a British soldier. Under such circumstances he is upheld, however, by the consideration that, while he is implicitly obeying the commands of his sovereign, to whom he has sworn fidelity, he purchases, by his blood, for his country, that internal peace and that supremacy of the law upon which alone are based the liberty as well as the permanent happiness and prosperity of a nation.

The regiment, originally sprung from those loyalists who had clung to Charles the Second in exile, has never failed in its duty to its Sovereign : it fought for James the Second against Monmouth on the field of Sedgemoor ; and struggled during five years heroically, although finally in vain, to preserve to George the Third his revolted American colonies.

Gentlemen! That same discipline which has made this regiment ever ready and terrible in war, has enabled it to pass long periods of peace

in the midst of all the temptations of a luxurious
metropolis without loss in vigour and energy,—
to live in harmony and good fellowship with its
brother citizens,—and to point to the remarkable fact, that the Household troops have now
for 200 years formed the permanent garrison of
London, have always been at the command of
the civil power to support law and order, but
have never themselves disturbed that order, or
given cause of complaint either by insolence or
licentiousness.

Let us hope that for centuries to come these
noble qualities may still shine forth, and that
the Almighty will continue to shield and favour
this little band of devoted soldiers; let us on
our part manfully do our duty, mindful of the
deeds of our predecessors, loyal to our Sovereign,
and jealous of the honour of our country.

I propose to you to drink " Prosperity to the
" Grenadier Guards, and to the health of Colonel
" Lewis, for so many years an honoured member
" of the corps, and now its zealous and able
" commander, and to the officers and men of the
" regiment."

3.

I have to propose to you " The Health of the

" Prince of Wales, and the other members of the
" Royal Family."

The Prince was admitted into the army a year
and a half ago, on his seventeenth birthday ; and
although his studies have as yet prevented his
taking upon himself any military duty, he has
while staying in Edinburgh tried to make himself acquainted with the evolutions of the cavalry
by joining regularly in the drill of the 16th
Lancers, quartered there at the time of his
residence.

4.

The toast I wish now to propose is that of our
sister-service—" The Navy."

The wooden walls of Old England have at all
times been the chief defence of our country, the
protection of our commerce, and constitute the
link which holds together our vast and widely
scattered empire.   Modern science has effected
greater changes in this service than perhaps in
any other human pursuit, and foreign nations
have, as it were, started afresh with us from the
same point of departure in the race of naval
preparation ; but there is in Englishmen that
confidence in their superiority on the unstable
element, which has powerful influence in cre-

ating and maintaining it, and gives assurance
of success. I believe at the same time the service never to have been in a higher state of
efficiency.

5.

Let us drink to " The Army."

That army, of which the brigade of Guards,
and this Regiment in it, form only a small but
integral part,—integral not only from its organization, but from its spirit and feeling. The
country has no less reason to be proud of its
Army than of its Navy; and if in point of
numbers it cannot boast of a supremacy, nay,
even a comparison with other countries, it yields
to none in those qualities of courage, discipline,
and endurance which constitute the essential
virtues of the soldier. The duties which this
army has to perform in peace as well as in war
could not, I make bold to say, be rendered by
any other army in the world; and although it
is a common doctrine that the British nation is
not a military nation, I totally disbelieve that
any other could furnish such an army, composed
entirely of volunteers as it is.

I beg to couple this toast with the health of
my dear relative, our gallant Commander-in-

Chief, who is indefatigable in his solicitude to maintain, and where possible to increase, its efficiency; and of the Queen's Secretary of State, who so ably presides over the civil administration of the Army, and has not only the sinews of war to prepare, but also that material by which science strives to reduce the individual power of man as an element in the attainment of victory, and on the superiority of which so much in war must in future depend.

"The Army, the Duke of Cambridge, and " Mr. Sidney Herbert."

6.

We are honoured by the presence of the Commanders of the other Regiments, both of cavalry and infantry, composing the Household Troops, whose services will live with yours in history, and render them worthy to be the body-guard of the Sovereign of these realms. We most painfully feel, however, the absence of one of these Commanders, whose name had been associated with the glories of the Guards in many a well-fought field. He has been called away from this temporary scene to an eternal and better world; but the memory of Sir John Byng (the Earl of Strafford) will ever be cherished by his brother officers.

The Scots Fusiliers, my personal connection with whom during ten years will always remain a proud and most pleasing recollection to me, will in a few days celebrate their jubilee as we are now doing; while the Coldstreams, true to their motto, have gained a march upon us in having had their jubilee some years before us, counting their creation from the time of the Commonwealth, when they formed General Monk's Regiment.

I beg to propose to you to drink the health of the Household Troops, and to connect with the toast the name of that gallant and distinguished general, Field Marshal Viscount Combermere.

TOAST GIVEN AT

THE DINNER OF THE TRINITY HOUSE.

[JUNE 23RD, 1860.]

1.

"THE QUEEN."

2.

I PROPOSE to drink to His Royal Highness the Prince of Wales and the rest of the Royal Family. The younger members of the Royal Family are rapidly growing up. The Princess Royal has already become the founder of a new family, destined to mount the throne of Prussia. The Prince of Wales is following his academic course at Oxford, which he intends to complete at the sister University, Cambridge; while his younger brother has, by the prescribed apprenticeship, earned his rating as Midshipman, and serves zealously as such in the Fleet. It will be a curious coincidence, that nearly at the same time—a few weeks hence—though almost at the opposite poles, the Prince of Wales will inaugurate, in the Queen's name, that stupendous work, the great bridge over the St. Lawrence in Canada, while Prince Alfred will lay the foundation stone of the breakwater for the harbour of Cape Town. What vast considerations, as regards our country, are brought to our minds in this simple fact! What present greatness! what past history! what future hopes! and how important and beneficent is the part given to the Royal Family of England to act in the development of those distant and rising countries, who recognize in the British Crown, and their allegiance to it, their supreme bond of union with the mother country and with each other!

3.

Gentlemen,—The standing toast, after that of the Royal Family, at all our public dinners, is "The Army and Navy;" and it is never given without calling forth proud and grateful feelings, for Englishmen have reason to be proud of the condition of these services, and of the deeds which they have achieved, and cause to be grateful for the benefits which have been secured to them by their soldiers and sailors, who have been

drawn from all ranks and classes of society, and
have devoted their lives to their country. We
hear sometimes complaints of the expense which
these services entail, and must certainly regret
that such sacrifices should be necessary; but on
the whole the public spirit with which the nation
is determined, through good and evil report, to
maintain the efficiency of these establishments, is
a most gratifying proof of its soundness at heart
and the shrewdness of its instinct. It has lately
come forward, and placed at the service of the
Queen, Volunteer Corps to act as an auxiliary to
the regular Army and Militia, in case of danger
to our shores; and the rapidity with which this
movement has developed itself has been the subject of universal and just admiration. We have
witnessed this day a scene which will never fade
from the memory of those who had the good
fortune to be present—the representatives of the
independence, education, and industry of this
country in arms, to testify their devotion to their
country, and their readiness to lay down their
lives in its defence. The Volunteer force ex-
ceeds already 130,000 men; and to what extent
this country is capable of exerting itself in real
danger is shown by the number of Volunteers,
which in 1804 reached the extraordinary figure

of 479,000! We are apt to forget, however,
that, in contrast with every other country of the
world, all our services are composed exclusively
of volunteers: the Navy, Coast-Guard, Coast
Volunteers, Army, Militia, Yeomanry, Con-
stabulary. May the noble and patriotic spirit
which such a fact reveals remain ever unim-
paired! And may God's blessing, of which this
nation has seen such unmistakable evidence,
continue to rest upon these voluntary services!
I beg to couple the toast with the names of the
First Lord of the Admiralty the Duke of Somer-
set, and Sir John Burgoyne.

4.

I am much obliged to you for your kindness in
drinking my health. I feel proud to have, by
the vote of this distinguished Corporation, been
re-elected its Master—an office of annual tenure,
which does not tax very hard the energies of the
holder, as the real work is admirably done by
the Deputy Master and the Elder Brethren; but
which is of the highest interest to whoever re-
flects upon the important and useful duties which
are performed by the Corporation, the proper
performance of which has so great an influence

on the commercial prosperity not only of this metropolis, but of the country at large.

I cannot meet you to-day without having one recalled to my memory who used to sit on my left hand on all former occasions, and who was honoured and beloved by this Corporation, and justly so, as its Deputy Master. Captain Shepheard was one of those unobtrusive but noble characters whose sterling qualities of head and heart secured to him the confidence of all who knew him ; and I can appeal to no greater proof of the estimation in which he was held than the fact that he was at once Deputy Master of this Corporation, Chairman of the East India Company, and Chairman of the Hudson's Bay Company. His successor, like himself, is an Aberdeenshire man, but, unlike him, has passed his life in the Royal Navy, and not the merchant service. I can wish him no better success than to possess the approbation of his brethren in an equal degree with his predecessor ! I propose to you to drink his health, and Prosperity to the Corporation of the Trinity House.

5.

We are honoured by the presence of Her Majesty's Ministers. The Corporation is much

gratified at their having found it possible, amidst
the many avocations and duties which so peculiarly press upon them during the Parliamentary
season, to devote an evening to the Trinity
House.   I propose to you to drink their health.
We can wish them nothing better than good
health, to enable them to withstand the fatigues
of their laborious and harassing life; and by
making the fullest use of their talents and energies, to gain that public recognition and confidence upon which so much of their success and
usefulness must depend.   This is not a political
meeting, and we cautiously abstain from alluding
to politics; whilst, therefore, the Ministers escape
our criticism, they must also forego our praise;
but we can give them what may be more valuable to them than either—the expression of our
esteem and good will.

"Lord Palmerston and Her Majesty's Minis-
"ters."

6.

We must not omit to acknowledge the presence of some of our Honorary Brethren, whose
admission to our body sheds lustre upon the Corporation.   The known presence of their names
upon our Roll gives the public an assurance that

we are well thought of and well looked after by some of the best in the land.

I beg to drink to the health of Lord Derby and the Honorary Brethren.

7.

Brethren of the Trinity House,—Let us, before separating, thank our guests for the honour they have done and the pleasure they have given us by their presence at our annual dinner; and let us drink to their health and happiness. I beg to couple this toast with the name of the Duke of Newcastle.

ON OPENING THE

INTERNATIONAL STATISTICAL CONGRESS.

[HELD IN LONDON, JULY 16TH, 1860.]

GENTLEMEN,—

THE Statistical Congress of All Nations has
been invited by the Government to hold
its fourth meeting in this metropolis, in con-
formity with the wishes expressed by the late
Congress held at Vienna in 1857. Although
under these circumstances it would have been
more properly within the province of a member
of the Government, and Minister of the Crown,
to fill this Chair, and open the proceedings of
the day, as has been the case in previous meetings of the Congress in other places, the nature
of the institutions and the habits of the people
of the country in which this Assembly was to
take place could not fail to make itself felt and
to influence its organization. We are a people
possessing and enjoying the most intense political life, in which every question of interest or

importance to the nation is publicly canvassed
and debated ; the whole nation, as it were, from
the highest to the lowest, takes an active part in
these debates, and arrives at a judgment with
regard to them, on the collective result of the
thoughts and opinions thus called forth.

This Congress could therefore only be either
a private meeting of the delegates of different
Governments, discussing special questions of
interest in the midst of the general bustle of
political activity, or it had to assume a public
and a national character, addressing itself to the
public at large, and inviting its co-operation.
The Government have chosen the latter alterna-
tive, and have been met by the readiest response
from all sides.   They have, I think, wisely
chosen ; for it is of the utmost importance to the
object the Congress has in view—namely, not
only the diffusion of statistical information, but
also the acquisition of a general acknowledgment
of the usefulness and importance of this branch
of human knowledge—that the public, as a
whole, should take up the questions which are
intended to be investigated, and should lend its
powerful aid.

Gentlemen, this explains, and must serve as
an apology for, my presuming to hold the post

s

of your President, for which I otherwise feel full well my unworthiness. When, however, the Commissioners for the organization of the Congress expressed to me their desire that I should do so, I felt it incumbent upon me not to withhold my individual co-operation, carrying with it, as it would, an assurance to the British people that the object of the Meeting was one which had enlisted the sympathy of their Queen, and testifying to the foreign delegates the esteem in which she holds them personally, and her appreciation of the science which they serve.

Let me now welcome them to this country, and welcome them on behalf of this country. It is here that the idea of an International Statistical Congress took its origin, when delegates and visitors from all nations had assembled to exhibit in noble rivalry the products of their science, skill, and industry, in the Great Exhibition of 1851; it is here that Statistical Science was earliest developed; and Dr. Farr has well reminded us that England has been called, by no less an authority than Bernouilli, " the cradle of poli-" tical arithmetic," and that we may even appeal to our Domesday Book as one of the most ancient and complete monuments of the science

in existence.   It is this country also which will
and must derive the greatest benefits from the
achievements of this science, and which will
consequently have most cause to be grateful to
you for the result of your labours.

Gentlemen, old as your science is, and undeniable as are the benefits which it has rendered
to mankind, it is yet little understood by the
multitude, new in its acknowledged position
amongst the other sciences, and still subject to
many vulgar prejudices.

It is little understood; for it is dry and unpa-
latable to the general public in its simple arith-
metical expressions, representing living facts
(which, as such, are capable of arousing the
liveliest sympathy) in dry figures and tables for
comparison.   Much labour is required to wade
through endless columns of figures, much patience to master them, and some skill to draw
any definite and safe conclusions from the mass
of material which it presents to the student;
while the value of the information offered depends exactly upon its bulk, increasing in
proportion with its quantity and comprehensiveness.

It has been little understood, also, from the
peculiar and often unjustifiable use which has

s 2

been made of it. For the very fact of its difficulty, and the patience required in reading up
and verifying the statistical figures which may
be referred to by an author in support of his
theories and opinions, protect him, to a certain
extent, from scrutiny, and tempt him to draw
largely upon so convenient and available a
capital. The public generally, therefore, connect in their minds statistics, if not with unwelcome taxation (for which they naturally form an
important basis), certainly with political contro-
versies, in which they are in the habit of seeing
public men making use of the most opposite
statistical results with equal assurance in support
of the most opposite arguments. A great and
distinguished French Minister and statesman is
even quoted as having boasted of the invention
of what he is said to have called "l'Art de
"grouper les Chiffres." But if the same ingenuity and enthusiasm which may have suggested
to him this art should have tempted him or others,
as historians, to group facts also, it would be no
more reasonable to make the historical facts
answerable for the use made of them than it
would be to make statistical science responsible
for many an ingenious financial statement.

Yet this science has suffered materially in

public estimation by such use, although the very
fact that statesmen, financiers, physicians, and
naturalists should seek to support their state-
ments and doctrines by statistics shows conclusively that they all acknowledge them as the
foundation of truth; and this ought, therefore,
to raise, instead of depressing, the science in the
general esteem of the public.

Statistical Science is, as I have said, comparatively new in its position amongst the sciences
in general; and we must look for the cause of
this tardy recognition to the fact that it has the
appearance of an incomplete science, and of
being rather a helpmate to other sciences than
having a right to claim that title for itself. But
this is an appearance only. For if pure statistics
abstain from participating in the last and highest
aim of all science (viz. the discovering and ex-
pounding the laws which govern the universe),
and leave this duty to their more favoured
sisters the natural and the political sciences, this
is done with conscious self-abnegation, for the
purpose of protecting the purity and simplicity
of their sacred task—the accumulation and veri-
fication of facts, unbiassed by any consideration
of the ulterior use which may, or can, be made
of them.

Those general laws, therefore, in the knowledge of which we recognize one of the highest treasures of man on earth, are left unexpressed, though rendered self-apparent, as they may be read in the uncompromising, rigid figures placed before him.

It is difficult to see how, under such circumstances, and notwithstanding this self-imposed abnegation, Statistical Science, as such, should be subject to prejudice, reproach, and attack; and yet the fact cannot be denied.

We hear it said that its prosecution leads necessarily to Pantheism, and the destruction of true religion, as depriving, in man's estimation, the Almighty of His power of free self-determination, making His world a mere machine working according to a general prearranged scheme, the parts of which are capable of mathematical measurement, and the scheme itself of numerical expression!—that it leads to fatalism, and therefore deprives man of his dignity, of his virtue and morality, as it would prove him to be a mere wheel in this machine, incapable of exercising a free choice of action, but predestined to fulfil a given task and to run a prescribed course, whether for good or for evil.

These are grave accusations, and would be

terrible indeed if they were true. But are they true? Is the power of God destroyed or diminished by the discovery of the fact that the earth requires three hundred and sixty-five revolutions upon its own axis to every revolution round the sun, giving us so many days to our year, and that the moon changes thirteen times during that period; that the tide changes every six hours; that water boils at a temperature of 212° according to Fahrenheit; that the nightingale sings only in April and May; that all birds lay eggs; that a hundred and six boys are born to every hundred girls? Or is man a less free agent because it has been ascertained that a generation lasts about thirty years; that there are annually posted at the Post-offices the same number of letters on which the writer had forgotten to place any address; that the number of crimes committed under the same local, national, and social conditions is constant; that the full-grown man ceases to find amusement in the sports of the child ?

But our Statistical Science does not even say that this must be so; it only states that it has been so, and leaves it to the naturalist or political economist to argue that it is probable, from

the number of times in which it has been found
to be so, that it will be so again, as long as the
same causes are operating. It thus gave birth
to that part of Mathematical Science called the
calculation of probabilities, and even established
the theory that in the natural world there exist
no certainties at all, but only probabilities. Although this doctrine, destroying man's feeling
of security to a certain extent, has startled and
troubled some, it is no less true that, whilst we
may reckon with a thoughtless security on the
sun rising to-morrow, this is only a probable
event, the probability of which is capable of
being expressed by a determined mathematical
fraction. Our insurance offices have, from their
vast collection of statistical facts, established, to
such a precision, the probable duration of man's
life, that they are able to enter with each individual into a precise bargain on the value of
this life ; and yet this does not imply an impious
pretension to determine when the individual is
really to die.

But we are met also by the most opposite objection ; and statistics are declared *useless*, because
they cannot be relied on for the determination
of any given cause, and do only establish probabilities where man requires and asks for cer-

tainty. This objection is well founded; but it does not affect the science itself, but solely the use which man has in vain tried to make of it, and for which it is not intended. It is the essence of the Statistical Science, that it only makes apparent general laws, but that these laws are inapplicable to any special case; that therefore what is proved to be law in general is uncertain in particular. Herein lies the real refutation also of the first objection; and thus is the power, wisdom, and goodness of the Creator manifested, showing how the Almighty has established the physical and moral world on unchangeable laws, conformable to His eternal nature, while He has allowed to the individual the freest and fullest use of his faculties, vindicating at the same time the majesty of His laws by their remaining unaffected by individual self-determination.

Gentlemen, I am almost ashamed to speak such homely truths (of which I feel myself at best to be a very inadequate exponent) to a meeting like this, including men of such eminence in the science, and particularly in the presence of one who was your first President, M. Quetelet, and from whom I had the privilege, now twenty-four years ago, to receive my first

instruction in the higher branches of mathematics—one who has so successfully directed
his great abilities to the application of the
science to those social phenomena, the discovery
of the governing laws of which can only be
approached by the accumulation and reduction
of statistical facts.

It is the social condition of mankind, as
exhibited by those facts, which forms the chief
object of the study and investigation undertaken
by this Congress; and it hopes that the results
of its labours will afford to the statesman and
legislator a sure guide in his endeavours to
promote social development and happiness.
The importance of these international Congresses
in this respect cannot be overrated. They not
only awaken public attention to the value of
these pursuits, bring together men of all countries
who devote their lives to them, and who are
thus enabled to exchange their thoughts and
varied experiences; but they pave the way to
an agreement amongst different governments
and nations to follow up these common inquiries,
in a common spirit, by a common method, and
for a common end.

It is only in the largest number of observations that the law becomes apparent; and the

truth becomes more and more to be relied upon,
the larger the amount of facts accurately observed
which form the basis of its elucidation. It is
consequently of the highest importance that
observations identical in character should embrace the largest field of observation attainable.
It is not sufficient, however, to collect the statistical
facts of one class, over the greatest area, and to
the fullest amount, but we require, in order to
arrive at sound conclusions as to the influences
operating in producing these facts, the simul-
taneous collection of the greatest variety of facts,
—the statistics of the increase of population,
of marriages, births and deaths, of emigration,
disease, crime, education and occupation, of the
products of agriculture, mining, and manufacture,
of the results of trade, commerce, and finance.
Nor, while their comparison becomes an essential
element in the investigation of our social condition, does it suffice to obtain these observations
as a whole, but we require also, and particularly,
the comparison of these same classes of facts in
different countries, under the varying influences
of political and religious conditions, of occupation, races, and climates. And even this comparison of the same facts in different localities
does not give us all the necessary material from

which to draw our conclusions; for we require, as much as anything else, the collection of observations of the same classes of facts, in the same localities, and under the same conditions, but at different times. It is only the element of time, in the last instance, which enables us to test progress or regress—that is to say, life.

Thus the physician, by feeling the pulse of the greatest number of individuals coming under his observation, old and young, male and female, and at all seasons, arrives at the average number of the pulsations of the heart in man's normal condition : by feeling the pulse of the same individual under the most varied circumstances and conditions, he arrives at a conclusion on this individual's pulse; again, by feeling the pulse of the greatest variety of persons suffering from the same disease, he ascertains the general condition of the pulse under the influence of that disease. It is only then that, feeling a particular patient's pulse, he will be able to judge whether this individual is affected by this peculiar disease, as far as that can be ascertained by its influence on the pulse.

But all these comparisons of the different classes of facts under different local conditions and at different times, of which I have been

speaking, depend, not only as to their usefulness
and as to the ease with which they can be undertaken, but even as to the possibility of undertaking them at all, on the similarity—nay,
congruity—of the method employed, and the
expressions, figures, and conditions selected,
under which the observations have been taken.
Does, then, the world at large not owe the
deepest obligations to a Congress such as the
one I am addressing, which has made it its
special task to produce this assimilation and to
place at the command of man the accumulated
experience upon his own condition, scientifically
elaborated and reduced in a manner to enable
the meanest intellect to draw safe conclusions?

Gentlemen, the Congress has at its various
meetings succeeded in doing a great deal in this
direction : the official statistics of all countries
have been improved ; and in regard to the
Census, the recommendations of the Brussels
meeting have been generally carried out in a
majority of States. I am sorry to have to admit
the existence of some striking exceptions in
England in this respect; for instance, the Census
of Great Britain and Ireland was not taken on
precisely the same plan in essential particulars,
thereby diminishing its value for general pur-

poses. The judicial statistics of England and Wales do not show a complete comparative view of the operation of our judicial establishments ; nor, while we are in all the departments of the State most actively engaged in the preparation of valuable statistics, can we deny certain defects in our returns, which must be traced to the want of such a central authority or Commission as was recommended by the Congress at Brussels and Paris, to direct, on a general plan, all the great statistical operations to be prepared by the various departments. Such a Commission would be most useful in preparing an annual digest of the Statistics of the United Kingdom, of our widely scattered Colonies, and of our vast Indian empire. From such a digest the most important results could not fail to be elicited.

One of the most useful results of the labours of the Congress has been the common agreement of all States to inquire into the causes of every death, and to return the deaths from the same causes under synonymous names, sanctioned by the Congress. It has in this instance set the example of establishing what is most desirable in all other branches of statistics, namely, the agreement upon well - defined terms. There ought to exist no greater difficulty in arriving at such an agreement in the case of the various crimes than in that of "causes of death;" and it must be remembered that it is one of the first tasks and duties of every science to start with a definition of terms. What is it that is meant by a house, a family, an adult, an educated or an uneducated person; by murder, manslaughter, and so on? It is evident that, as long as a different sense is attached to these terms in different returns, their use for comparison is nil, and for simple study very much deteriorated; and still we have not yet arrived at such a simple and obvious desideratum! The different weights, measures, and currencies in which different statistics are expressed, cause further difficulties and impediments. Suggestions with regard to the removal of these have been made at former meetings, and will no doubt be renewed. We fancy here that our Pound, as the largest available unit, with its Florin, offers great advantages, particularly if further sub-divided decimally.

We hope to lay before you, as far as Great Britain is concerned, the Registrar-General's analysis of the causes of death, and the dangers that people encounter at each period of life; complete returns of the produce of our mines;

the agricultural returns of Ireland, in which the Registrar-General of that country has given every year the breadth of land under every kind of crop, with an estimate of its produce as well as its value, and has proved, by his success in obtaining these facts at a comparatively moderate expense, and by the voluntary assistance of the landowners and cultivators, as well as of the clergy of all denominations, that the apprehension was groundless that it could not be done without inordinate cost, or without injuring individual interests.   We must hope that, considering its importance with regard to all questions affecting the food of the people, this inquiry will not only be extended to England and Scotland, but also to the Continent generally, wherever it may not already have been instituted.   Our trade returns will exhibit the great effects produced on our commerce by the changes in our commercial system ; our colonial delegates will exhibit to you proofs of the wonderful progress of their countries, and proofs, at the same time, that elaborate statistics have rendered them conscious of that progress ; and I have no doubt that the foreign delegates. will more than repay us by the information which they will give us in exchange.   These returns will no doubt prove to us afresh, in figures, what we know already from feeling and from experience—how dependent the different nations are upon each other for their progress, for their moral and material prosperity, and that the essential condition of their mutual happiness is the maintenance of peace and good-will amongst each other. Let them still be rivals, but rivals in the noble race of social improvement, in which, although it may be the lot of one to arrive first at the goal, yet all will equally share the prize, all feeling their own powers and strength increase in the healthy competition.

I should detain you longer than I feel justified in doing, and should perhaps trench upon the domain and duties of Presidents of Sections, if I were to allude to the points which will there be specially recommended to your attention and consideration ; but I trust that it will not be thought presumptuous in me if I exhort you generally not to lose yourselves in points of minute detail, however tempting and attractive they may be from their intrinsic interest and importance, but to direct your undivided energies to the establishment of those broad principles upon which the common action of different nations can be based, which common action

T

must be effected, if we are to make real progress. I know that this Congress can only suggest and recommend, and that it must ultimately rest with the different Governments to carry out those suggestions. Many previous recommendations, it is true, have been carried out, but many have been left unattended to; and I will not except our own country from blame in this respect. Happy and proud indeed should I feel if this noble gathering should be enabled to lay the solid foundation of an edifice, necessarily slow of construction, and requiring, for generations to come, laborious and persevering exertion, intended as it is for the promotion of human happiness, by leading to the discovery of those eternal laws upon which that universal happiness is dependent!

May He, who has implanted in our hearts a craving after the discovery of truth, and given us our reasoning faculties to the end that we should use them for this discovery, sanctify our efforts and bless them in their results!

LONDON: PRINTED BY W. CLOWES AND SONS, STAMFORD STREET,
AND CHARING CROSS.

For EU product safety concerns, contact us at Calle de José Abascal, 56–1°,
28003 Madrid, Spain or eugpsr@cambridge.org.

www.ingramcontent.com/pod-product-compliance
Ingram Content Group UK Ltd.
Pitfield, Milton Keynes, MK11 3LW, UK
UKHW010344140625
459647UK00010B/807